W9-ALU-490

# 500
# Quick & Easy
## Recipes

igloobooks

igloobooks

*Published in 2016*
*by Igloo Books Ltd*
*Cottage Farm*
*Sywell*
*NN6 0BJ*
*www.igloobooks.com*

*Copyright© 2013 Igloo Books Ltd*

*HUN001 0916*
*4 6 8 10 9 7 5 3*
*ISBN 978-1-78343-221-9*

*Food photography and recipe development: PhotoCuisine UK*
*Front and back cover images © PhotoCuisine UK*

*Printed and manufactured in China*

# CONTENTS

# STARTERS AND SIDES

# 1

**SERVES 4**

# Goats' Cheese Potato Cakes

## Goats' Cheese and Chorizo Potato Cakes

2

- Fry 100 g / 3 ½ oz / ½ cup cubed chorizo in 2 tbsp olive oil before adding it to the potato and goats' cheese mixture.

## Feta and Cumin Potato Cakes

3

- Replace the goats' cheese with crumbled feta and replace the chives with ½ tsp ground cumin.

PREPARATION TIME 20 MINUTES

COOKING TIME 8 MINUTES

### INGREDIENTS

300 g / 10 ½ oz / 2 cups left over boiled potatoes, cold
1 egg yolk
salt and pepper
100 g / 3 ½ oz / ⅔ cup goats' cheese, cubed
2 tbsp fresh chives, chopped
1 tbsp flat leaf parsley, chopped
50 g / 1 ¾ oz / ⅓ cup panko breadcrumbs
4 tbsp olive oil

### TO SERVE
1 beefsteak tomato
small handful of rocket (arugula) leaves
a few sprigs parsley and chives
1 tbsp olive oil

- Mash the potato with the egg yolk and plenty of salt and pepper then knead in the goats' cheese and herbs.
- Divide the mixture into 4 and shape it into patties. Dip the potato cakes in the breadcrumbs to coat.
- Heat the oil in a large frying pan and fry the potato cakes for 4 minutes on each side or until golden brown.
- Meanwhile, cut 4 large slices from the middle of the tomato and cut the ends into cubes.
- Put a tomato slice in the centre of each plate and arrange the rocket, cubed tomato and herbs round the outside.
- Drizzle the salad with oil then position a potato cake on top of each tomato slice.

**SERVES 4**

# Cheese Goujons

- Cut the cheese into fingers with a sharp knife.
- Put the flour, egg and panko breadcrumbs in 3 separate bowls.
- Dip the cheese first in the flour, then in egg, then in the breadcrumbs to coat thoroughly.
- Heat the oil in a deep fat fryer, according to the manufacturer's instructions, to a temperature of 180°C.
- Lower the goujons in the fryer basket and cook for 4–5 minutes or until crisp and golden brown.
- Line a large bowl with a thick layer of kitchen paper and when they are ready, tip them into the bowl to remove any excess oil.
- Sprinkle with a little sea salt to taste and serve immediately.

PREPARATION TIME 15 MINUTES

COOKING TIME 4–5 MINUTES

### INGREDIENTS

400 g / 14 oz / 3 ½ cups Emmental or Gouda
4 tbsp plain (all purpose) flour
1 egg, beaten
75 g / 2 ½ oz / ½ cup panko breadcrumbs
2–3 litres / 3 ½ pints–5 pints / 8–12 cups sunflower oil
sea salt

## Deep-fried Camembert

- Replace the cheese fingers with wedges of Camembert. Serve with redcurrant sauce.

**SERVES 4**

# Sautéed Potatoes with Cumin

- Boil the potatoes in salted water for 8 minutes then drain well and leave to steam dry for 2 minutes.
- Heat the oil in a large sauté pan.
- Sprinkle the potatoes with cumin, thyme and plenty of salt and pepper then fry for 10 minutes, shaking the pan and stirring occasionally.

PREPARATION TIME 5 MINUTES

COOKING TIME 18 MINUTES

### INGREDIENTS

800 g / 1 lb 12 oz / 5 ⅓ cups charlotte potatoes, halved or quartered
4 tbsp olive oil
1 tsp ground cumin
2 tbsp fresh thyme leaves

## Sautéed Potatoes with Garlic and Rosemary

- Break 1 bulb of garlic into cloves and boil in their skins with the potatoes before sautéing. Leave out the cumin and replace the thyme with chopped fresh rosemary.

**SERVES 4**

# Stuffed Mushrooms

PREPARATION TIME 4 MINUTES

COOKING TIME 15 MINUTES

## INGREDIENTS

8 anchovy fillets
100 g / 3 ½ oz / ⅔ cup mascarpone
1 clove garlic, crushed
1 tbsp chives, chopped
1 tbsp flat leaf parsley, chopped
4 large mushrooms, destalked

- Preheat the oven to 200°C (180°C fan) / 390F / gas 6.
- Finely chop 4 of the anchovy fillets and mix them with the mascarpone, garlic and half the herbs.
- Divide the mixture between the mushroom cavities and place on a baking tray. Bake for 15 minutes until the mushrooms have softened and the topping is lightly coloured.
- Top each mushroom with a whole anchovy fillet and sprinkle with the remaining herbs.

## Bacon Stuffed Mushrooms

9

- Replace the anchovies with 4 rashers of crispy streaky bacon.

**SERVES 4**

# Oven-baked Vegetables

PREPARATION TIME 5 MINUTES

COOKING TIME 45 MINUTES

## INGREDIENTS

4 baby artichokes, trimmed and halved
½ cauliflower, broken into florets
1 stick of celery, chopped
1 courgette (zucchini), cut into batons
8 mushrooms, sliced
4 tomatoes, cubed
2 tbsp fresh thyme leaves
2 cloves garlic, unpeeled and bruised
4 tbsp olive oil
salt and pepper

- Preheat the oven to 200°C (180°C fan) / 390 F / gas 6.
- Mix all the vegetables with the thyme, garlic and olive oil and layer in a baking dish.
- Season well with salt and pepper then bake for 45 minutes, stirring every 15 minutes.

## Baked Chicken and Vegetables

11

- Add 4 chicken thighs, quartered, to the vegetables and cook as before.

**MAKES 12**

# Mini Herb Frittatas

- Preheat the oven to 180°C (160°C fan) / 355 F / gas 4.
- Lightly beat the eggs and mix them with the onion and herbs then season well with salt and pepper.
- Pour the mixture into a 12-hole silicone cupcake mould and bake in the oven for 15–20 minutes or until the frittatas are set in the centre.
- Serve warm or at room temperature.

PREPARATION TIME 5 MINUTES

COOKING TIME 15–20 MINUTES

### INGREDIENTS

6 eggs
½ red onion, finely chopped
2 tbsp flat leaf parsley, finely chopped
2 tbsp chives, finely chopped
2 tbsp basil, finely chopped
salt and pepper

### Mini Breakfast Frittatas

 13

- Chop 2 cooked rashers of streaky bacon and 1 cooked sausage and stir them into the eggs in place of the onions and herbs.

**SERVES 4**

# Fresh Broad Bean Salad

- Put the shallots in a bowl with the vinegar, sugar and a big pinch of salt and leave to macerate for 10 minutes.
- Meanwhile, blanch the broad beans in boiling water for 5 minutes then drain and refresh in cold water. Drain well.
- Whisk the olive oil into the shallot vinegar and taste for seasoning then stir in the chervil and broad beans.

PREPARATION TIME 10 MINUTES

COOKING TIME 5 MINUTES

### INGREDIENTS

2 shallots, finely chopped
3 tbsp sherry vinegar
2 tsp caster (superfine) sugar
salt
600 g / 1 lb 5 oz / 5 ½ cups fresh broad beans, podded weight
4 tbsp extra virgin olive oil
a small bunch chervil, chopped

### Green Bean Salad

 15

- Replace the broad beans with 400 g / 14 oz / 2 ½ cups of trimmed green beans.

16

SERVES 4

# Vegetable Kebabs

## Halloumi and Vegetable Kebabs

17

- Marinate 300 g / 10 oz / 2 cups of cubed Halloumi cheese with the vegetables.

## Spicy Vegetable Kebabs

18

- Replace the herbes de Provence with 1 tbsp harissa paste.

PREPARATION TIME 25 MINUTES

COOKING TIME 8 MINUTES

.....................................................

### INGREDIENTS

1 tbsp dried herbes de Provence
3 tbsp olive oil
1 red pepper, deseeded and cubed
1 green pepper, deseeded and cubed
1 large courgette (zucchini), thickly sliced
½ aubergine (eggplant), cubed
100 g / 3 ½ oz / 1 ⅓ cups button mushrooms, thickly sliced
4 salad onions, halved

### FOR THE DIP

1 tbsp lemon juice
½ tsp cracked black pepper
4 tbsp mayonnaise

- Put 12 wooden skewers in a bowl of water and leave to soak for 20 minutes.
- Meanwhile, stir the herbs into the oil and toss it with the vegetables.
- Leave to marinate for 20 minutes.
- Meanwhile, make the dip by stirring the lemon juice and black pepper into the mayonnaise.
- Preheat the grill to its highest setting.
- Thread alternate vegetables onto the skewers and spread them out on a large grill tray.
- Grill the kebabs for 4 minutes on each side or until they are golden brown and cooked through.

**MAKES 6**

# Warm Scotch Eggs

- Put 6 of the eggs in a pan of cold water then bring to a simmer and cook for 5 minutes.
- Cool, then peel off the shells.
- Skin the sausages and divide the meat into 6. Flatten a portion of sausage meat onto your hand and put an egg in the centre, then squeeze the meat round the outside to coat. Repeat with the other 5 eggs.
- Put the flour, remaining egg and panko breadcrumbs in 3 separate bowls.
- Dip the scotch eggs first in the flour, then in egg, then in the breadcrumbs.
- Heat the oil in a deep fat fryer, according to the manufacturer's instructions, to a temperature of 180°C.
- Lower the scotch eggs in the fryer basket and cook for 4–5 minutes or until crisp and golden brown.
- Sprinkle with a little sea salt and serve immediately.

## Black Pudding Scotch Eggs

 20

- Halve the quantity of sausages and mix with 200 g / 7 oz / ¾ cup of crumbled black pudding.

PREPARATION TIME 30 MINUTES

COOKING TIME 10 MINUTES

**INGREDIENTS**

7 small eggs
4 good quality pork sausages
4 tbsp plain (all purpose) flour
75 g / 2 ½ oz / ½ cup panko breadcrumbs
2–3 litres / 3 ½–5 pints / 8–12 cups sunflower oil
sea salt

 21

**SERVES 4**

# Ham and Mushroom Savoury Pancakes

- Preheat the oven to 200°C (180°C fan) / 390F / gas 6.
- Melt the butter in a large saucepan and fry the mushrooms with a pinch of salt for 5 minutes.
- Stir in the flour then gradually incorporate the milk, stirring continuously to avoid any lumps forming.
- When the mixture starts to bubble, stir in the ham and a grind of black pepper then take the pan off the heat.
- Lay the pancakes out on the work surface and divide the mushroom mixture between them.
- Roll the pancakes up and transfer them to a baking tray then bake for 10 minutes or until golden brown.

## Three-cheese Savoury Pancakes

22

- Replace the ham and mushrooms with 75 g / 2 ½ oz / ¾ cup each of cubed mozzarella, finely grated Parmesan and cubed Gorgonzola.

PREPARATION TIME 5 MINUTES

COOKING TIME 20 MINUTES

**INGREDIENTS**

50 g / 1 ¾ oz / ¼ cup butter
200 g / 7 oz / 2 cups button mushrooms, chopped
salt and pepper
1 tbsp plain (all purpose) flour
300 ml / 10 ½ fl. oz / 1 ⅓ cups milk
100 g / 3 ½ oz / ⅔ cup ham, chopped
8 ready-made pancakes

23

SERVES 4

# Spicy Prawn and Green Bean Salad

PREPARATION TIME 5 MINUTES

COOKING TIME 4 MINUTES

## INGREDIENTS

200 g / 7 oz / 2 cups green beans, trimmed
1 clove garlic, crushed
½ tsp Cayenne pepper
3 tbsp olive oil
12 raw king prawns (shrimps), peeled leaving tails intact
1 tbsp lemon juice
30 g / 1 oz / ⅓ cups Parmesan shavings
4 sprigs coriander (cilantro)
salt and pepper

- Preheat the grill to its highest setting.
- Blanch the beans in boiling salted water for 4 minutes or until al dente. Plunge into cold water and drain well.
- Meanwhile, mix the garlic and Cayenne with 1 tablespoon of the oil and massage the paste into the prawns.
- Spread the prawns out on a grill tray and grill for 2 minutes on each side or until only just opaque.
- Mix the rest of the oil with the lemon juice and season well with salt and pepper.
- Toss the dressing with the beans then top with the prawns.
- Use a vegetable peeler to shave some Parmesan over the top and garnish with coriander.

### Prawn and Bean Salad

24

- Omit the Parmesan. Make a dressing using 1 tbsp caster sugar, 1 tbsp fish sauce and juice of 1 lime. Stir in ½ tsp of finely chopped garlic and ½ tsp red chilli before dressing.

25

SERVES 4

# Melon, Feta and Mint Salad

PREPARATION TIME 5 MINUTES

## INGREDIENTS

1 small white or green-fleshed melon, halved
1 small orange-fleshed melon, halved
100 g / 3 ½ oz / ⅔ cup feta, finely cubed
4 tbsp mint leaves, shredded
4 tbsp extra virgin olive oil
salt and pepper

- Use a melon baller to scoop small balls out of the melons and toss them with the feta and mint.
- Drizzle with olive oil then sprinkle with sea salt and freshly ground black pepper.

### Melon, Goats' Cheese and Basil Salad

26

- Replace the feta with an equal quantity of goats' cheese and replace the mint with shredded basil.

**27**

**SERVES 2**

# Feta and Cherry Tomato Salad

- Arrange the lettuce leaves on 2 plates and top with the feta, tomatoes and olives.
- Drizzle with olive oil and sprinkle with pink peppercorns.

PREPARATION TIME 5 MINUTES

### INGREDIENTS

6 large lettuce leaves
100 g / 3 ½ oz / ⅔ cup feta, cubed
6 cherry tomatoes, quartered
a few kalamata olives
4 tbsp extra virgin olive oil
½ tsp pink peppercorns, crushed

## Greek Salad

 **28**

- Cut half a cucumber into cubes and toss with the feta, olives and tomatoes.

**29**

**SERVES 2**

# Potato and Antipasti Salad

- Boil the potatoes in salted water for 12 minutes or until tender in the middle, then plunge into cold water to stop the cooking and drain well.
- Toss the potatoes with the vegetable antipasti and dress with 2 tablespoons of the oil.
- Use a vegetable peeler to shave over some Parmesan and garnish with basil. Season with salt and black pepper.

PREPARATION TIME 2 MINUTES

COOKING TIME 12 MINUTES

### INGREDIENTS

300 g / 10 ½ oz / 2 cups Maris Piper potatoes, peeled and thickly sliced
1 jar mixed vegetable antipasti in oil, drained and oil reserved
30 g / 1 oz / ⅓ cups Parmesan
a few sprigs basil
salt and pepper

## Potato and Preserved Octopus Salad

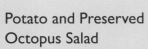 **30**

- Replace the mixed antipasti with 200 g / 7 oz / 1 ⅓ cups canned octopus pieces in oil. Squeeze the juice of a lemon over the finished salad before serving.

31

SERVES 4

# Fusilli with Mixed Vegetables

PREPARATION TIME 2 MINUTES

COOKING TIME 12 MINUTES

.................................................

## INGREDIENTS

400 g / 14 oz / 5 cups fusilli pasta
4 tbsp olive oil
4 cloves garlic, crushed
1 red pepper, deseeded and cubed
½ head broccoli, broken into small florets
1 carrot, shredded
1 courgette (zucchini), shredded

- Cook the fusilli in boiling salted water according to the packet instructions or until al dente.
- While the pasta is cooking, heat the olive oil in a large frying pan and cook the garlic, peppers and broccoli for 5 minutes, stirring occasionally.
- Add the shredded carrot and courgette to the pan and cook for 2 more minutes.
- Reserve 1 ladle of the pasta cooking water and drain the rest then stir the pasta into the frying pan.
- If it looks a bit dry, add some of the cooking water and shake the pan to emulsify.
- Divide the pasta between 4 warm bowls and serve.

32

SERVES 4

# Fusilli with Olives and Artichokes

PREPARATION TIME 2 MINUTES

COOKING TIME 12 MINUTES

.................................................

## INGREDIENTS

400 g / 14 oz / 5 cups mixed fusilli and penne pasta
4 tbsp olive oil
4 cloves garlic, crushed
1 red pepper, deseeded and cubed
1 jar preserved baby artichokes, drained
75 g / 3 oz / ½ cup green olives, pitted
75 g / 3 oz / ½ cup black olives, pitted and sliced

- Cook the pasta in boiling salted water according to the packet instructions or until al dente.
- While the pasta is cooking, heat the olive oil in a large frying pan and cook the garlic and peppers for 5 minutes, stirring occasionally.
- Stir in the artichokes and olives and warm through.
- Reserve 1 ladle of the pasta cooking water and drain the rest then stir the pasta into the frying pan.
- If it looks a bit dry, add some of the cooking water and shake the pan to emulsify.
- Divide the pasta between 4 warm bowls and serve.

**33**

**SERVES 4**

# Couscous Salad

- Put the couscous in a large serving bowl and pour over 300 ml of boiling water.
- Cover the bowl with clingfilm and let it stand for 5 minutes then fluff up the grains with a fork.
- Stir through the peppers, tomato and mint.
- Whisk the honey with the lemon juice then whisk in the olive oil.
- Pour the dressing over the couscous and serve.

PREPARATION TIME 5 MINUTES

COOKING TIME 5 MINUTES

### INGREDIENTS

300 g / 10 ½ oz / 1 ¾ cup couscous
1 red pepper, deseeded and cubed
1 green pepper, deseeded and cubed
1 tomato, deseeded and cubed
2 tbsp mint, chopped

FOR THE DRESSING
1 tsp runny honey
½ lemon, juiced
3 tbsp olive oil

**34**

**SERVES 4**

# Salad Niçoise

PREPARATION TIME 5 MINUTES

COOKING TIME 12 MINUTES

### INGREDIENTS

400 g / 14 oz / 2 ⅔ cup charlotte potatoes, halved
1 oak leaf lettuce, leaves separated
1 jar white tuna in olive oil, drained
and cubed
6 tomatoes, quartered
75 g / 2 ½ oz / ½ cup black olives, pitted
4 tbsp extra virgin olive oil
a few sprigs chervil to garnish

- Boil the potatoes in salted water for 12 minutes or until tender, then drain well.
- Arrange the lettuce on 4 serving plates and arrange the tuna, potatoes, tomatoes and olives on top.
- Drizzle with olive oil and garnish with chervil.

**35**

**SERVES 4**

# Chef's Salad

PREPARATION TIME 8 MINUTES

### INGREDIENTS

1 lettuce, separated into leaves
½ cucumber, peeled and sliced
2 tomatoes, cut into wedges
1 stick celery, chopped
1 hard-boiled egg, quartered

100 g / 3 ½ oz / 1 cup Emmental, cut into sticks
1 cooked chicken breast, cut into strips
100 g / 3 ½ oz / ⅔ cup ham, cubed

FOR THE DRESSING
1 tsp Dijon mustard
1 tsp runny honey, 1 lemon, juiced
3 tbsp olive oil

- Line 4 serving bowls with lettuce leaves and arrange the cucumber, tomato and celery on top.
- Add a boiled egg quarter to each bowl and divide the cheese, chicken and ham between them.
- Put the dressing ingredients in a jar with a pinch of salt and pepper and shake to emulsify.
- Drizzle the dressing over the salad and serve immediately.

**36**
**SERVES 4**

# Roast Chicken and Boiled Egg Salad

PREPARATION TIME 15 MINUTES

**INGREDIENTS**

a small bunch of radishes, trimmed
1 lettuce, separated into leaves
½ cucumber, sliced
2 tomatoes, cut into wedges
1 stick celery, chopped
2 hard-boiled eggs, quartered
75 g / 3 oz / ½ cup black olives, pitted
2 skin-on roasted chicken breasts, sliced
mayonnaise, to serve

- Slit the ends of the radishes and put them in a bowl of iced water for 5 minutes to fan out.
- Line a large serving bowl with lettuce leaves and arrange the cucumber, tomato and celery on top.
- Add a ring of boiled egg quarters and radishes round the outside and put the chicken in the middle.
- Scatter over the olives and serve with a bowl of mayonnaise on the side.

### Poached Salmon Salad
 **37**

- Replace the chicken with 300 g / 10 oz / 2 cups cold flaked poached salmon fillet.

**38**
**SERVES 4**

# Imam Bayildi

PREPARATION TIME 10 MINUTES

COOKING TIME 30 MINUTES

**INGREDIENTS**

6 tbsp olive oil
1 onion, finely chopped
4 cloves garlic, crushed
1 tbsp sesame seeds
3 tomatoes, skinned, deseeded and finely chopped
1 tbsp mint, finely chopped
1 tbsp flat leaf parsley, finely chopped
2 aubergines (eggplant), sliced

- Heat 2 tablespoon of the oil in a sauté pan and fry the onion for 5 minutes. Add the garlic and sesame seeds and cook for 2 more minutes.
- Stir in the tomatoes, mint and parsley and simmer gently for 15 minutes, adding a little water if it gets too dry.
- Meanwhile, brush the aubergines with 4 tablespoons of the oil and season with salt and pepper.
- Fry them in batches for 3 minutes on each side or until golden brown and tender. Keep the cooked aubergines warm in a low oven while you cook the rest.
- Divide the aubergines between 4 plates and layer up with the tomato sauce.

### Aubergine with Preserved Lemon
 **39**

- Cut 1 lemon into quarters and remove the flesh. Finely chop the zest and stir it into the tomato sauce before layering with the aubergine slices.

**40**

**SERVES 2**

# Marinated Anchovies with Tomato Salsa

- Score a cross in the top of the tomatoes and blanch in boiling water for 30 seconds. When the skin of the tomatoes starts to curl up, remove them with a slotted spoon and dunk in a bowl of cold water.
- Peel off and discard the skins then cut them in half and remove the seeds. Chop the tomato flesh into small cubes.
- Mix the herbs with the olive oil, a pinch of salt and plenty of freshly ground black pepper.
- Arrange the anchovy fillets on 2 plates and spoon some of the herb oil on top.
- Stir the rest of the herb oil into the chopped tomatoes and divide between the 2 plates.

PREPARATION TIME 10 MINUTES

COOKING TIME 1 MINUTE

### INGREDIENTS

2 medium tomatoes
1 tbsp fresh basil leaves, chopped
1 tbsp flat leaf parsley, chopped
1 tsp fresh young rosemary, finely chopped
4 tbsp extra virgin olive oil
16 marinated anchovy fillets

### Grilled Sardines with Tomato Salsa

 **41**

- This salsa also works realy well with fresh sardines, lightly grilled or barbecued.

**42**

**SERVES 4**

# Cucumber Salad

- Crush the peppercorns and chilli flakes with a pestle and mortar then add the garlic and a pinch of salt and grind to a paste.
- Add the lemon juice, stirring with the pestle, followed by the oil, then stir in the yoghurt.
- Spoon the mixture into a serving bowl and toss with the cucumber and herbs.

PREPARATION TIME 5 MINUTES

### INGREDIENTS

½ tsp mixed peppercorns
a pinch chilli (chili) flakes
½ clove garlic
1 tbsp lemon juice
2 tbsp olive oil
3 tbsp Greek yoghurt
1 cucumber, cut into batons
a small bunch chives, chopped
a small bunch flat leaf parsley, chopped

### Cucumber and Beetroot Salad

 **43**

- Cut 3 small cooked and peeled beetroots into batons and combine with the cucumber and dressing.

19

**44**

**SERVES 4**

# Prosciutto-wrapped Halloumi Kebabs

### Prosciutto-wrapped Chicken Kebabs

**45**

- Replace the Halloumi with 300 g / 10 oz / 2 ⅓ cups cubed skinless chicken breast.

### Prosciutto-wrapped Salmon Kebabs

**46**

- Replace the Halloumi with 300 g / 10 oz / 2 ⅓ cups cubed skinless salmon fillet.

PREPARATION TIME 20 MINUTES

COOKING TIME 8 MINUTES

### INGREDIENTS

300 g / 10 ½ oz / 2 ½ cups Halloumi, cubed
150 g / 5 ½ oz / 1 cup prosciutto
28 cherry tomatoes
2 shallots, quartered
12 bay leaves, halved

- Put 12 wooden skewers in a bowl of water and leave to soak for 20 minutes.
- Preheat the grill to its highest setting.
- Wrap each Halloumi cube in prosciutto then thread them onto the skewers with the tomatoes, shallots and bay leaves.
- Grill the kebabs for 4 minutes on each side or until they are golden brown and warmed through.

47

SERVES 2

# Griddled Courgettes

- Preheat a griddle pan until smoking hot.
- Brush the courgette slices with half of the oil and griddle for 2 minutes on each side or until nicely marked.
- Transfer the courgettes to 2 warm serving plates, drizzle with the rest of the olive oil and sprinkle with sea salt. Garnish with oregano.

PREPARATION TIME 2 MINUTES

COOKING TIME 4 MINUTES

### INGREDIENTS

2 courgettes (zucchini), sliced
lengthways
2 tbsp olive oil
2 sprigs oregano
sea salt

## Griddled Aubergine

48

- Substitute the courgettes (zucchini) with a sliced aubergine (eggplant).

49

SERVES 4

# Chicken and Fruit a la Plancha

- Put 12 wooden skewers in a bowl of water and leave to soak for 20 minutes.
- Meanwhile, stir the spices into the oil and toss with the chicken and fruit.
- Leave to marinate for 20 minutes.
- Preheat a plancha (cast iron skillet) to its highest setting.
- Thread the chicken pieces onto the skewers spread them out on the plancha. Arrange the fruit around the sides and cook everything for 4 minutes on each side or until the chicken is cooked through.

PREPARATION TIME 30 MINUTES

COOKING TIME 8 MINUTES

### INGREDIENTS

½ tsp ground white pepper
½ tsp ground coriander (cilantro)
4 tbsp olive oil
6 skinless chicken breasts, cubed
½ pineapple, skin on, cut into wedges
2 red apples, cut into chunks

## Prawns and Mango a la Plancha

50

- Replace chicken breasts with 300 g / 10 oz / 2 ⅓ cups raw king prawns and marinate as above. Substitute fruit with a mango that has been peeled, stoned and cut into fingers.

## 51
**SERVES 4**

# Lamb's Liver Kebabs with Tomato Sauce

PREPARATION TIME 20 MINUTES

COOKING TIME 30 MINUTES

### INGREDIENTS

1 tbsp rosemary, finely chopped
2 tbsp olive oil
450 g / 1 lb / 3 cups lamb's liver, cubed
1 green pepper, deseeded and cubed
1 red pepper, deseeded and cubed
1 yellow pepper, deseeded and cubed
salt

FOR THE SAUCE
4 tbsp olive oil
1 onion, sliced
2 cloves garlic, crushed
400 g / 14 oz / 2 ⅓ cup canned tomatoes, chopped

- Put 8 wooden skewers in a bowl of water and leave to soak for 20 minutes.
- Meanwhile, stir the rosemary into the oil and toss it with the liver and peppers.
- Leave to marinate for 20 minutes.
- Meanwhile, heat the oil in a sauté pan and fry the onion for 5 minutes to soften. Add the garlic and cook for 2 more minutes, then stir in the tomatoes. Simmer for 15 minutes.
- Preheat the grill to its highest setting.
- Thread alternate chunks of liver and pepper onto the skewers and spread them out on a large grill tray.
- Sprinkle with salt and grill for 4 minutes on each side or until they are golden brown and cooked through.
- Serve 2 skewers per person with a small bowl of tomato sauce.

### Kidney and Mushroom Kebabs  ## 52

- Substitute the liver with an equal weight of kidney and the peppers with 250 g / 9 oz / 1 ⅔ cups button mushrooms.

## 53
**SERVES 4**

# Griddled Vegetables on Toast

PREPARATION TIME 5 MINUTES

COOKING TIME 6 MINUTES

### INGREDIENTS

1 courgette (zucchini), sliced lengthways
1 aubergine (eggplant), sliced lengthways
4 tbsp olive oil
salt and pepper
8 slices sourdough bread
8 sun-dried tomatoes in oil, drained
a few sprigs basil

- Preheat a griddle pan until smoking hot.
- Brush the courgette and aubergine slices with the oil and season with salt and pepper.
- Griddle the vegetables for 3 minutes on each side or until nicely marked.
- Toast the sourdough and divide the slices between 4 plates.
- Arrange the vegetables on top with the sun-dried tomatoes and garnish with basil.

### Griddled Vegetables and Halloumi on Toast  ## 54

- Cut a 200 g block of Halloumi into slices and griddle with the vegetables before arranging on top of the toast.

**55**

SERVES 4

# Goats' Cheese, Tomato and Basil Crostini

## Goats' Cheese, Peach and Basil Crostini

**56**

- Replace the sliced tomatoes with wedges of fresh peach.

## Goats' Cheese and Prosciutto Crostini

**57**

- Replace the tomato with thin slices of prosciutto and replace the basil with fresh young thyme leaves.

PREPARATION TIME 10 MINUTES

COOKING TIME 10 MINUTES

.......................................................

### INGREDIENTS

12 slices wholemeal baguette
4 tbsp olive oil
200 g / 7 oz / 1 ⅓ cups fresh goats' cheese
2 tbsp basil, finely chopped
2 tomatoes, sliced
12 sprigs basil
salt and pepper

- Preheat the oven to 200⁰C (180⁰C fan) / 390 F / gas 6.
- Brush the baguette slices with half of the oil and spread them out on a baking tray. Bake for 10 minutes or until crisp.
- Meanwhile, put the goats' cheese, chopped basil and the rest of the oil in a bowl with plenty of freshly ground black pepper. Mash it to a paste with a fork.
- When the crostini are ready, spread them with the goat's cheese mixture and top each one with a slice of tomato and a sprig of basil.

**58**

SERVES 4

# Pea and Potato Purée with Croutons

PREPARATION TIME 8 MINUTES

COOKING TIME 15 MINUTES

......................................................

## INGREDIENTS

600 g / 1 lb 5 ½ oz / 4 cups potatoes, peeled and cubed
400 g / 14 oz / 4 cups frozen peas, defrosted
250 ml / 9 fl. oz / 1 cup whole milk
150 g / 5 ½ oz / ⅔ cup butter, cubed
salt and pepper
a few sprigs chervil to garnish

## FOR THE HALLOUMI CROUTONS

200 g / 7 oz / 2 cups Halloumi, cubed
½ tsp ground cumin
½ tsp ground coriander (cilantro) seeds
2 tbsp olive oil

- Put the potatoes in a pan of cold, salted water and bring to the boil.
- Cook for 10 minutes then add the peas. Continue to cook until the potatoes are tender all the way through.
- Tip the vegetables into a colander and leave to drain.
- Put the saucepan back on the heat and add the milk and butter.
- Heat until the milk starts to simmer then return the potatoes and peas to the pan.
- Take the pan off the heat and purée with a stick blender then season to taste with salt and pepper.
- Meanwhile, toss the Halloumi with the spices and fry in the oil for 2 minutes on each side or until golden brown.
- Remove the Halloumi from the pan with a slotted spoon and sprinkle over the puree with the chervil.

### Minted Pea and Potato Purée

**59**

- Add 1 tbsp of chopped fresh mint leaves to the pan before pureeing.

**60**

SERVES 4

# Red Cabbage and Orange Salad

PREPARATION TIME 15 MINUTES

......................................................

## INGREDIENTS

2 oranges
½ lemon, juiced
3 tbsp olive oil
salt and pepper
½ red cabbage, shredded
50 g / 1 ¾ oz / ⅓ cup roasted cashew nuts

- Cut a slice off the end of each orange, then stand them on end and slice off and discard the peel in strips.
- Use a sharp knife to cut out each individual segment, leaving the pith behind like the pages of a book.
- Reserve the orange segments and squeeze the pith into a bowl to collect the juices. Discard the pith.
- Add the lemon juice to the bowl and whisk in the olive oil with a good pinch of salt and pepper.
- Add the red cabbage to the bowl and toss well to coat. Leave to stand for 10 minutes to soften the cabbage slightly then stir again.
- Combine the cabbage with the orange segments and cashews and serve immediately.

### Red Cabbage and Grapefruit Salad

**61**

- Substitute the oranges with grapefruits and use walnuts in place of the cashews.

**62**

**SERVES 4**

# Red Cabbage and Apple Salad

- Whisk together the lemon juice, olive oil and coriander seeds and toss with the cabbage.
- Leave to stand for 10 minutes for the cabbage to soften then stir in the apple slices and season.

**PREPARATION TIME 12 MINUTES**

### INGREDIENTS

1 lemon, juiced
4 tbsp olive oil
1 tsp coriander (cilantro) seeds, crushed
½ red cabbage, shredded
1 apple, cored and very thinly sliced
salt and pepper

### Red Cabbage, Pear and Stilton Salad

**63**

- Use pears, and crumble in 100 g / 3 ½ oz / ½ cup of Stilton at the end.

**64**

**SERVES 2**

# Broccoli and Bacon Salad

- Heat 1 tablespoon of the oil in a frying pan and fry the bacon for 3 minutes on each side or until crisp.
- Meanwhile, blanch the broccoli in boiling salted water for 3–4 minutes or until just tender. Drain well.
- While the bacon and broccoli are cooking, whisk the honey and mustard into the vinegar with a pinch of salt then incorporate the rest of the oil.
- Toss the drained broccoli with the dressing and split between 2 serving plates.
- Lay 2 rashers of bacon on top of each plate and use a vegetable peeler to shave over some Parmesan.

**PREPARATION TIME 2 MINUTES**

**COOKING TIME 12 MINUTES**

### INGREDIENTS

3 tbsp olive oil
4 rashers streaky bacon
1 small head broccoli, broken into small florets
1 tsp runny honey
1 tsp Dijon mustard
1 tbsp balsamic vinegar
salt
30 g / 1 oz / ½ cup Parmesan

### Broccoli, Chilli and Anchovy Salad

**65**

- Omit the bacon and add 4 chopped anchovy fillets and a finely chopped red chilli (chili) to the dressing.

## 66
**SERVES 2**

# Brie and Tomato Toasts

PREPARATION TIME 5 MINUTES

COOKING TIME 10–12 MINUTES

### INGREDIENTS

4 slices sourdough bread
8 slices Brie
1 tomato, thinly sliced
1 tbsp fresh thyme leaves
a handful rocket (arugula) leaves
olive oil, to drizzle
black pepper

- Preheat the grill to its highest setting.
- Toast the slices of sourdough on one side under the grill.
- Turn them over and top each one with the brie, tomatoes and a sprinkle of thyme.
- Grill for 2 more minutes or until the cheese is bubbling and the bread is toasted at the edges.
- Serve 2 toasts per plate with some rocket on the side. Drizzle some olive oil over the rocket and sprinkle everything with freshly ground black pepper.

### Brie and Roasted Pepper Toasts 67
- Replace the tomatoes with a jar of roasted peppers in oil and use some of the oil from the jar to dress the rocket.

## 68
**SERVES 4**

# Sole and Mushroom Skewers with Rice

PREPARATION TIME 20 MINUTES

COOKING TIME 26 MINUTES

### INGREDIENTS

200 g / 7 oz / 1 cup mixed basmati, red and wild rice
450 g / 1 lb / 3 cups sole, filleted and cut into strips
200 g / 7 oz / 2 cups button mushrooms, halved
2 tbsp olive oil
salt
fresh coriander (cilantro) sprigs to garnish

- Put 16 wooden skewers in a bowl of water and leave to soak for 20 minutes.
- Meanwhile, put the rice in a saucepan and add enough water to cover it by 1 cm (½ in).
- Bring the pan to the boil then cover and turn down the heat to its lowest setting.
- Cook for 10 minutes then turn off the heat and leave to stand, without lifting the lid, for 10 minutes.
- Preheat the grill to its highest setting.
- Roll up the sole fillets and thread them onto the skewers with the mushrooms. Brush the skewers with oil and spread them out on a large grill tray.
- Sprinkle with salt and grill for 3 minutes on each side or until they are golden brown and cooked through.
- Fluff up the rice with a fork then divide it between 4 warm plates then top with the kebabs and coriander.

### Sole and Prawn Skewers with Rice 69
- Replace the mushrooms with 150 g / 5 oz / 1 cup of raw peeled king prawns.

**70**

**SERVES 3**

# Bacon-wrapped Scallop Kebabs

### Scallop, Bacon and Tomato Kebabs

**71**

- Substitute the mushrooms with cherry tomatoes and garnish with parsley instead of coriander.

### Bacon-wrapped Monk Fish Kebabs

**72**

- Replace the scallops with a cubed monkfish tail.

PREPARATION TIME 20 MINUTES

COOKING TIME 8 MINUTES

.......................................................

## INGREDIENTS

12 scallops
6 rashers streaky bacon, halved
12 button mushrooms
1 lime, cut into wedges
fresh coriander (cilantro) leaves to garnish

- Put 6 wooden skewers in a bowl of water and leave to soak for 20 minutes.
- Preheat the grill to its highest setting.
- Wrap the scallops in bacon then thread them onto the skewers with the mushrooms.
- Grill the kebabs for 4 minutes on each side or until they are golden brown and garnish with lime and coriander.

73

SERVES 4

# Duck and Mango Salad

## Chilli Duck and Mango Salad

74

- Add a finely chopped red chilli (chili) and a crushed clove garlic to the dressing before spooning it over the salad.

## Duck and Pineapple Salad

75

- Replace the mango with half a diced fresh pineapple.

PREPARATION TIME 10 MINUTES

COOKING TIME 5 MINUTES

### INGREDIENTS

1 large skinless duck breast, cut into thin strips
2 tbsp peanuts
1 tbsp vegetable oil
¼ Chinese cabbage, chopped
1 under-ripe mango, julienned
a small bunch of mint, leaves only
4 spring onions (scallions), sliced

FOR THE DRESSING
1 tbsp caster (superfine) sugar
1 tbsp fish sauce
2 limes, juiced
1 tsp sesame oil

- Stir-fry the duck and peanuts in the vegetable oil for 5 minutes or until cooked through.
- Toss the duck with the cabbage, mango, mint and spring onions.
- Mix together the dressing ingredients and spoon them over the top.

**SERVES 2** 76

# Chicory and Ham Salad

- Toss the chicory leaves with the radishes, melon, ham, cheese and nuts.
- Whisk the orange juice and olive oil together with a pinch of salt and pepper and drizzle it over the salad.

PREPARATION TIME 12 MINUTES

### INGREDIENTS

2 heads chicory (endive), separated into leaves
4 radishes, sliced
¼ white-fleshed melon, peeled and sliced
50 g / 1 ¾ oz / ⅓ cup cooked ham, cut into matchsticks
50 g / 1 ¾ oz / ½ cup Gouda, cubed
50 g / 1 ¾ oz / ⅓ cup walnuts, chopped

### FOR THE DRESSING
½ orange, juiced
1 tbsp olive oil
salt and pepper

### Chicory and Roquefort Salad
 77
- Omit the ham and radishes and replace the Gouda with Roquefort.

**SERVES 4** 78

# Lentil, Green Bean and Asparagus Salad

- Cook the lentils in simmering, unsalted water for 20–30 minutes or until tender, but still holding their shape.
- Drain well and plunge into cold water to stop the cooking. Drain well.
- While the lentils are cooking, blanch the green beans in boiling salted water for 4 minutes or until al dente. Plunge into cold water and drain well.
- Meanwhile, make the dressing. Whisk the honey into the lemon juice then incorporate the oil. Season to taste with salt and pepper, then stir in the basil.
- Top the lentils with the beans and asparagus tips then spoon over the dressing.

PREPARATION TIME 8 MINUTES

COOKING TIME 30 MINUTES

### INGREDIENTS

400 g / 14 oz / 2 ⅔ cup red lentils
100 g / 3 ½ oz / ⅔ cup green beans
1 jar green asparagus tips, drained

### FOR THE DRESSING
1 tsp runny honey
2 tbsp lemon juice
4 tbsp olive oil
salt and pepper
2 tbsp basil leaves, shredded

### Puy Lentil and Asparagus Salad
 79
- Replace the red lentils with Puy lentils. Use 200 g / 7 oz / 1 cup of fresh asparagus instead of the jar. Brush it with olive oil and griddle for 6 minutes, turning occasionally.

**80**

SERVES 4

# Moroccan Chicken Salad

PREPARATION TIME 35 MINUTES

## INGREDIENTS

½ tsp ground turmeric
½ tsp ground cumin
½ tsp ground cinnamon
2 tsp runny honey
2 tbsp lemon juice
4 tbsp olive oil
2 cooked chicken breasts, cut into chunks
200 g / 7 oz / 1 ⅓ cup boiled potatoes, cooled
2 baby preserved lemons, halved
12 green olives
8 cherry tomatoes, halved

- Whisk the spices, honey and lemon juice into the oil.
- Mix the chicken with the potatoes, preserved lemons, olives and tomatoes and pour over the dressing.
- Leave to infuse for 30 minutes then divide between 4 bowls and serve.

## Moroccan Squash Salad

**81**

- For a vegetarian version of this dish, replace the chicken with 300 g / 10 ⅓ oz / 2 cups of roasted butternut squash chunks.

**82**

SERVES 4

# Rice Salad with Orange and Figs

PREPARATION TIME 5 MINUTES

COOKING TIME 20 MINUTES

## INGREDIENTS

200 g / 7 oz / 1 ¼ cup long grain rice
½ cucumber, sliced
1 orange, peeled and sliced
4 dried figs, chopped
6 dried apricots, sliced
1 tbsp pistachios, chopped
2 tbsp chives, chopped
salt and pepper

FOR THE DRESSING
1 tsp runny honey
½ lemon, juiced
3 tbsp olive oil

- Put the rice in a saucepan and add enough water to cover it by 1 cm.
- Bring the pan to the boil then cover and turn down the heat to its lowest setting.
- Cook for 10 minutes then turn off the heat and leave to stand, without lifting the lid, for 10 minutes.
- Whisk the honey with the lemon juice then whisk in the olive oil.
- When the rice is ready, combine it with the rest of the ingredients and dressing and season well with salt and pepper.
- Serve warm or at room temperature.

## Rice Salad with Grapefruit and Dates

**83**

- Replace the orange segments with grapefruit segments and replace the figs with chopped, stoned dates.

**84**

**SERVES 4**

# Chicken, Tomato and Nasturtium Salad

- Arrange the chicken, tomatoes and spring onions on 4 plates and sprinkle over the thyme.
- Drizzle with olive oil and season with salt and pepper then garnish with the nasturtiums.

PREPARATION TIME 5 MINUTES

.............................................

## INGREDIENTS

2 cooked chicken breasts, sliced
200 g / 7 oz / 1 ⅓ cup cherry tomatoes, halved
200 g / 7 oz / 2 cups / 1 ⅓ cup yellow cherry tomatoes, halved
4 spring onions (scallions), sliced lengthways
2 tbsp thyme leaves
4 tbsp extra virgin olive oil
salt and pepper
a handful of nasturtium flowers

### Mozzarella, Tomato and Nasturtium Salad

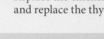 85

- Replace the chicken with 2 sliced mozzarella balls and replace the thyme with shredded basil leaves.

**86**

**SERVES 4**

# Prawn and Grapefruit Stir-fry

- Stir the chilli, garlic and coriander into the oil then pour it over the prawns and leave to marinate for 15 minutes.
- Heat a wok until smoking hot then add the prawns, mange tout and peas and stir-fry until the prawns turn opaque.
- Stir in the soy sauce and pink grapefruit and serve immediately.

PREPARATION TIME 5 MINUTES

COOKING TIME 4 MINUTES

.............................................

## INGREDIENTS

1 red chilli (chili), finely chopped
1 clove garlic, crushed
1 tbsp coriander (cilantro) leaves, finely chopped
3 tbsp olive oil
20 raw king prawns (shrimps), peeled leaving tails intact
200 g / 7 oz / 2 cups mange tout, trimmed
100 g / 3 ½ oz / 1 cup frozen peas, defrosted
1 tbsp soy sauce
1 pink grapefruit, cut into segments

### Prawn, Broccoli and Grapefruit Stir-fry

 87

- Replace the mange tout with ½ a head of broccoli, broken into small florets.

**88**

SERVES 4

# Green Bean, Bacon and Cheese Salad

## Green Bean, Bacon and Chicken Salad

**89**

- Omit the cheese and fry 1 cubed chicken breast with the bacon until cooked through.

## Green Bean, Bacon and Caper Salad

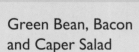

**90**

- Replace the cheese with 1 tbsp of capers.

PREPARATION TIME 5 MINUTES

COOKING TIME 6 MINUTES

................................................

### INGREDIENTS

200 g / 7 oz / 2 cups green beans, trimmed, sliced diagonally
6 rashers smoked bacon, sliced
2 tbsp olive oil
black pepper
2 tbsp white wine vinegar
150 g / 5 ½ oz / 1 ½ cup mild Cheddar, cubed

- Blanch the beans in boiling salted water for 4 minutes or until al dente. Plunge into cold water and drain well.
- Meanwhile, fry the bacon in the oil for 4 minutes or until crisp.
- While the bacon is cooking, toss the cheese with some freshly ground black pepper.
- When the bacon is ready, remove it from the pan with a slotted spoon and toss it with the beans and cheese.
- Add the vinegar to the pan to deglaze and spoon it over the salad as a dressing.

**91**

**SERVES 6**

# Provençal Anchovy Salad

- Boil the potatoes in salted water for 12 minutes or until tender, then drain well.
- Meanwhile, blanch the beans in boiling salted water for 4 minutes then plunge into cold water and drain well.
- Toss the potatoes, beans, cucumber, peppers and shallots with 8 of the boiled egg quarters and the tuna.
- Arrange the anchovies on top and scatter over the olives then arrange the tomato wedges and remaining boiled egg quarters round the outside.
- Whisk the oil and vinegar together with a good grind of salt and pepper and drizzle it over the salad just before serving.

PREPARATION TIME 10 MINUTES

COOKING TIME 12 MINUTES

......................................................

**INGREDIENTS**

400 g / 14 oz / 2 ⅔ cup charlotte potatoes, peeled and sliced
200 g / 7 oz / 2 cups green beans, halved
½ cucumber, sliced
1 yellow pepper, deseeded and sliced
1 shallot, thinly sliced
3 hard-boiled eggs, quartered
50 g / 1 ¾ oz / ⅓ cup white tuna in olive oil, drained and flaked
50 g / 1 ¾ oz / ⅓ cup anchovy fillets in olive oil, drained
50 g / 1 ¾ oz / ⅓ cup black olives, pitted
1 tomato, cut into wedges
4 tbsp extra virgin olive oil
2 tbsp white wine vinegar
salt and pepper

## Provencal Steak Salad

**92**

- Brush a large sirloin steak with olive oil and cook in a hot griddle pan for 3 minutes on each side, then slice thinly and mix with the rest of the salad ingredients.

**93**

**SERVES 2**

# Asparagus with Scrambled Egg and Feta

- Snap the woody ends off the asparagus and cut the spears in half. Steam the asparagus for 5 minutes or until tender.
- Heat the olive oil in a large sauté pan and add the eggs. Stir continuously until they start to scramble then add the asparagus to the pan and stir-fry for 2 more minutes.
- Stir in the feta and sesame seeds then serve immediately, garnished with basil.

PREPARATION TIME 5 MINUTES

COOKING TIME 10 MINUTES

......................................................

**INGREDIENTS**

200 g / 7 oz / 2 cups fresh asparagus
4 tbsp olive oil
2 eggs, beaten
100 g / 3 ½ oz / ⅔ cup feta, cubed
1 tbsp sesame seeds
a few sprigs basil

## Asparagus with Feta and Sesame Dressing

 **94**

- Follow the recipe above but omit the scrambled eggs.

95

SERVES 4

# Baby Octopus and Pepper Salad

PREPARATION TIME 30 MINUTES

COOKING TIME 8 MINUTES

## INGREDIENTS

3 tbsp olive oil
1 red pepper, deseeded and diced
1 orange pepper, deseeded and diced
1 yellow pepper, deseeded and sliced
1 green pepper, deseeded and diced
2 cloves garlic, finely chopped
300 g / 10 ½ oz / 2 cups baby octopus, cleaned
2 tbsp flat leaf parsley, chopped

## FOR THE DRESSING

2 tbsp olive oil
2 tbsp double (heavy) cream
1 lemon, juiced
2 tsp Dijon mustard
1 tsp runny honey

- Put all of the dressing ingredients in a jar and shake well to emulsify.
- Heat the oil in a large sauté pan and fry the peppers with the garlic for 5 minutes or until softened.
- Add the octopus and parsley and cook for 2 minutes over a very high heat until just opaque.
- Pour over the dressing and turn off the heat.
- Leave for 30 minutes for the octopus to cool and absorb the flavour of the dressing before serving.

## Baby Octopus and Red Onion Salad

 96

- Replace the peppers with 2 sliced red onions. Fry with the garlic for 10 minutes before adding the octopus.

97

SERVES 4

# Curry-fried Potatoes

PREPARATION TIME 2 MINUTES

COOKING TIME 18 MINUTES

## INGREDIENTS

800 g / 1 lb 12 oz / 5 ⅓ cups charlotte potatoes, peeled and sliced
4 tbsp olive oil
1 onion, sliced
3 tsp mild curry powder
lime slices and coriander (cilantro) leaves, to garnish

- Boil the potatoes in salted water for 8 minutes then drain well and leave to steam dry for 2 minutes.
- Heat the oil in a large sauté pan and fry the onion for 4 minutes.
- Add the potatoes and curry powder and stir-fry for 4 minutes or until golden.
- Transfer to a hot serving plate and garnish with lime and coriander.

## Curry-fried Sweet Potato

98

- Replace the potatoes with sweet potatoes, but reduce the boiling time to 6 minutes.

**99**

**SERVES 2**

# Sautéed Potatoes, Courgettes and Feta

- Boil the potatoes in salted water for 8 minutes then drain well and leave to steam dry for 2 minutes.
- Heat 4 tbsp of the oil in a large sauté pan.
- Season the potatoes with plenty of salt and pepper then fry for 10 minutes, shaking the pan and stirring occasionally.
- Add the courgette slices and stir-fry for 2 more minutes then stir in the feta and chives and serve immediately.

PREPARATION TIME 2 MINUTES

COOKING TIME 25 MINUTES

**INGREDIENTS**

6 tbsp olive oil
400 g / 14 oz / 2 ⅔ cups charlotte potatoes, peeled and cubed
salt and pepper
1 courgette (zucchini), halved and thinly sliced
100 g / 3 ½ oz / ⅔ cup feta, cubed
a small bunch chives, chopped

## Sautéed Potatoes, Peppers and Feta

**100**

- Omit the courgette and add 2 julienned red peppers when you start frying the potatoes.

**101**

**SERVES 4**

# Tuna Sashimi and Tomato Salad

- Score a cross in the top of the tomatoes and blanch them in boiling water for 30 seconds. When the skin of the tomatoes starts to curl up, remove them with a slotted spoon and dunk in a bowl of cold water.
- Peel off and discard the skins then finely chop the tomato flesh. Mix together the mirin, vinegar, sugar and sesame oil and use it to dress the tomatoes.
- Use a sharp knife to trim the tuna into 6 cm x 3 cm (2 in x 1 in) fillets, then cut it across the grain into 1 cm (½ in) slices.
- Slice the avocado and onion and arrange everything on 4 serving plates.

PREPARATION TIME 20 MINUTES

COOKING TIME 30 SECONDS

**INGREDIENTS**

200 g / 7 oz / 1 ⅓ cup sushi-grade tuna loin
1 avocado, peeled and stoned
1 red onion, peeled and halved

FOR THE TOMATO SALAD

6 tomatoes
1 tbsp rice wine (mirin)
1 tbsp rice vinegar
1 tsp caster (superfine) sugar
1 tsp sesame oil

## Sashimi Medley

**102**

- Follow the method above to cut sushi-grade salmon and sea bass into sashimi as well.

103

SERVES 2

# Almond and Olive Tapenade Crostini

## Salsa Verde Crostini

104

- Omit the almonds and add 3 tbsp each of chopped flat leaf parsley and basil.

## Black Olive Tapenade Crostini

105

- Omit the almonds and mint and replace the green olives with stoned kalamata olives.

PREPARATION TIME 10 MINUTES

COOKING TIME 4 MINUTES

### INGREDIENTS

2 tbsp blanched almonds
100 g / 3 ½ oz / ⅔ cup green olives, pitted
3 tbsp capers
1 clove garlic, crushed
2 tbsp mint leaves, torn
2 tbsp olive oil
2 slices white bread
sun-dried tomatoes and basil, to serve

- Put the almonds, olives and capers on a chopping board and chop them all together until coarsely chopped and evenly mixed.
- Scrape the mixture into a bowl and stir in the garlic, mint and oil then season to taste with salt and pepper.
- Toast the bread, cut into triangles, then spread the tapenade on top.
- Serve with some sun-dried tomatoes and basil on the side.

## 106
**SERVES 2** Pear, Brie and Hazelnut Toasts

- Preheat a griddle pan until smoking hot.
- Brush the bread with oil then toast it in the griddle pan for 4 minutes, turning every minute.
- Meanwhile, melt the butter in a frying pan and fry the pear slices for 4 minutes or until softened and golden.
- Arrange the pears on top of the toast and top with the Brie and hazelnuts. Sprinkle over a little cinnamon and serve immediately.

PREPARATION TIME 5 MINUTES

COOKING TIME 4 MINUTES

### INGREDIENTS

1 slice wholemeal bread, halved diagonally
2 tbsp olive oil
1 tbsp butter
1 pear, peeled, cored and sliced
2 slices ripe Brie
2 tbsp hazelnuts (cob nuts), roughly chopped
½ tsp ground cinnamon

### Pear and Brioche Toasts

107

- For a sweet version of this dish, replace the bread with brioche and omit the brie in favour of a drizzle of honey.

## 108
**SERVES 4** Smoked Scamorza Toasts

- Preheat the grill to its highest setting.
- Toast the slices of sourdough on one side under the grill.
- Turn them over and top each one with the cheese and a sprinkle of thyme.
- Grill for 2 more minutes or until the cheese is bubbling and the bread is toasted at the edges.

PREPARATION TIME 2 MINUTES

COOKING TIME 4 MINUTES

### INGREDIENTS

4 slices sourdough bread
200 g / 7 oz / 2 cups smoked Scamorza or mozzerella
½ tsp dried thyme

### Smoked Scamorza and Tomato Toasts

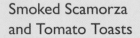

109

- Mix 6 quartered cherry tomatoes with the cheese and thyme before arranging on top of the bread.

# Stir-fried Noodles with Vegetables

**110**

**SERVES 4**

**PREPARATION TIME 5 MINUTES**

**COOKING TIME 15 MINUTES**

## INGREDIENTS

200 g / 7 oz / 2 ⅔ cup thin egg noodles
3 tbsp vegetable oil
1 courgette (zucchini), halved and sliced
½ aubergine (eggplant), sliced
½ jar sun-dried tomatoes in oil, drained
2 cloves garlic, crushed
flat leaf parsley, to garnish

- Cook the noodles in boiling salted water according to the packet instructions or until al dente, then drain well.
- Heat the oil in a large wok and fry the courgette and aubergine for 5 minutes or until browned.
- Add the sun-dried tomatoes and garlic and stir-fry for 2 minutes then add the drained noodles and stir-fry for a final minute.
- Divide between 4 warm bowls and serve, garnished with parsley.

### Stir-fried Noodles with Oyster Sauce

**111**

- Omit the tomatoes and add a sliced red pepper to the wok when you fry the courgette and aubergine. Add 3 tbsp of oyster sauce to the wok when you add the noodles.

# Cherry Tomato Gratin

**112**

**SERVES 4**

**PREPARATION TIME 10 MINUTES**

**COOKING TIME 30 MINUTES**

## INGREDIENTS

2 slices stale sourdough bread
1 clove garlic, finely chopped
½ tsp smoked paprika
a small bunch parsley, leaves only
salt and pepper
400 g / 14 oz / 2 ⅔ cup cherry tomatoes
3 tbsp olive oil

- Preheat the oven to 200°C (180°C fan) / 390F / gas 6.
- Tear the bread into chunks and put it in a food processor with the garlic, paprika and half of the parsley.
- Pulse until roughly chopped then season with salt and pepper.
- Arrange the tomatoes in a baking dish and sprinkle the breadcrumb mixture over the top.
- Drizzle with olive oil then bake for 30 minutes or until golden brown.
- Divide between 4 warm bowls and scatter over the rest of the parsley.

### Tomato and Mozzarella Gratin

**113**

- Add 150 g / 5 oz / ⅔ cup of cubed mozzarella to the cherry tomatoes before sprinkling over the breadcrumbs.

**114**

**SERVES 4**

# Red Mullet and Coppa Crostini

- To make the salsa, stir the grapefruit, shallot and parsley together then whisk in the oil. Season to taste with salt and pepper.
- Heat the oil in a large frying pan. Season the red mullet fillets with salt and pepper and wrap each one in half a sheet of Coppa.
- Fry the fish, skin side down, for 2 minutes.
- Turn the fillets over then turn off the heat and leave them to cook in the heat of the pan for 1 minute.
- While the fish is cooking, toast the bread.
- Arrange the mullet on top of the crostini and drizzle over the salsa. Garnish with mixed salad leaves.

**PREPARATION TIME 10 MINUTES**

**COOKING TIME 4 MINUTES**

.......................................................

### INGREDIENTS

2 tbsp olive oil
8 red mullet fillets
4 slices Coppa ham, halved
8 slices baguette
mixed salad leaves to serve

### FOR THE SALSA

4 grapefruit segments, skinned and chopped
1 shallot, finely chopped
1 tbsp flat leaf parsley, finely chopped
2 tbsp extra virgin olive oil
salt and pepper

### Sea Bass and Prosciutto Crostini

**115**

- Replace the red mullet with 4 sea bass fillets, cut in half diagonally. Replace the coppa with prosciutto.

**116**

**SERVES 2**

# Pickled Herring and Vegetables

- Toast the ciabatta slices and top with the sun-dried tomatoes and aubergine then lay a herring fillet on top of each one.
- Mix the garlic and chervil with the vinegar and oil and drizzle it over the top, then garnish with chervil sprigs.

**PREPARATION TIME 10 MINUTES**

**COOKING TIME 4 MINUTES**

.......................................................

### INGREDIENTS

4 slices ciabatta
4 pickled herring fillets
1 jar sun-dried tomatoes in oil, drained
1 jar preserved aubergines (eggplants) in oil, drained
½ clove garlic, crushed
1 tbsp chervil, finely chopped, plus extra sprigs to garnish
1 tsp white wine vinegar
1 tbsp olive oil

### Pickled Herring and Coleslaw Toasts

**117**

- Replace the preserved vegetables and dressing with 4 tbsp of coleslaw.

118

SERVES 4

# Spinach and Walnut Bruschetta

### Spinach and Stilton Bruschetta

119

- Replace the goats' cheese with an equal quantity of Stilton.

### Florentine Bruschetta

120

- Omit the goats' cheese and walnuts and add a poached egg to the top of each bruschetta.

PREPARATION TIME 4 MINUTES

COOKING TIME 4 MINUTES

....................................................

### INGREDIENTS

100 g / 3 ½ oz / 1 ⅓ cups baby leaf spinach
4 slices walnut bread
1 clove garlic, halved
2 tbsp walnut oil
50 g / 1 ¾ oz / ⅓ cup goats' cheese, cubed
2 tbsp walnuts, roughly chopped

- Heat a saucepan on the hob and wash the spinach, then put it in the pan and cover with a lid.
- Let it steam for 2 minutes, then tip it into a sieve to drain off any excess liquid.
- Toast the walnut bread then rub with the halved garlic clove and drizzle with walnut oil.
- Arrange the hot spinach on top and dot over the cheese and walnuts.

**121**

**SERVES 4**

# Yakitori Chicken

- Put 16 wooden skewers in a bowl of water and leave to soak for 20 minutes.
- Meanwhile, mix together the mirin, sake, soy and sugar and massage it into the chicken pieces.
- Leave to marinate for 20 minutes.
- Prepare a barbecue or heat a griddle pan until smoking hot.
- Thread the chicken onto the skewers then cook them for 4 minutes on each side or until they are golden brown and cooked through.

PREPARATION TIME 25 MINUTES

COOKING TIME 8 MINUTES

.........................................................

### INGREDIENTS

1 tbsp rice wine (mirin)
1 tbsp sake
1 tbsp soy sauce
2 tsp caster (superfine) sugar
8 boneless chicken thighs, cubed

## Yakitori Pork Belly

**122**

- Replace the chicken thighs with 450 g / 1 lb / 3 cups of cubed skinless pork belly.

**123**

**SERVES 4**

# Coddled Eggs with Bacon and Shallots

- Preheat the oven to 180°C (160°C fan) / 355F / gas 4.
- Fry the bacon and shallot in the oil for 2 minutes then stir in the tarragon and crème fraiche.
- Divide half the mixture between 4 ramekin dishes and crack an egg into each one, then top with the rest of the crème fraiche mixture.
- Put the ramekins in a roasting tin and add enough boiling water to the tin to come half way up the side of the ramekins.
- Bake for 15 minutes or until the eggs are cooked to your liking, then serve immediately.

PREPARATION TIME 5 MINUTES

COOKING TIME 18 MINUTES

.........................................................

### INGREDIENTS

2 rashers smoked streaky bacon, thinly sliced
1 shallot, halved and thinly sliced
1 tbsp olive oil
1 tbsp tarragon, chopped
150 g / 5 ½ oz / ⅔ cup crème fraiche
4 large eggs

## Eggs with Smoked Salmon

 **124**

- Omit bacon and shallots and add 75 g / 2 ½ oz / ½ cup of chopped smoked salmon when you stir in the tarragon.

## 125

**SERVES 1**

# Halloumi and Parsley Omelette

PREPARATION TIME 5 MINUTES

COOKING TIME 6 MINUTES

### INGREDIENTS

3 large eggs
salt and pepper
2 tbsp flat leaf parsley
1 tbsp butter
50 g / 1 ¾ oz / ½ cup Halloumi, cubed
½ tsp pink peppercorns, crushed

- Break the eggs into a jug with a pinch of salt and pepper and beat them gently to break up the yolks.
- Stir in the parsley and Halloumi.
- Heat the butter in a non-stick frying pan until sizzling then pour in the eggs.
- Cook over a medium heat until the eggs start to set around the outside. Use a spatula to draw the sides of the omelette into the centre and tilt the pan to fill the gaps with more liquid egg.
- Repeat the process until the top of the omelette is just set then sprinkle over the pink peppercorns.

### Tofu and Parsley Omelette

126

- Replace the Halloumi with cubed firm tofu that has been fried until golden in a little olive oil.

## 127

**SERVES 4**

# Creamy Tomato Soup

PREPARATION TIME 10 MINUTES

COOKING TIME 30 MINUTES

### INGREDIENTS

400 g / 14 oz / 2 ½ cups tomatoes
2 tbsp olive oil
1 onion, finely chopped
2 cloves garlic, crushed
1 tbsp tomato puree
1 L / 1 pint 15 fl. oz / 4 cups vegetable stock
2 tbsp crème fraiche
salt and pepper
2 tbsp flat leaf parsley, chopped

- Score a cross in the top of the tomatoes and blanch them in boiling water for 30 seconds.
- Plunge them into cold water then peel off the skins.
- Cut the tomatoes in half and remove the seeds, then cut the flesh into small cubes.
- Heat the oil in a saucepan and fry the onion for 5 minutes or until softened. Add the garlic and cook for 2 more minutes then stir in the tomatoes and tomato puree.
- Pour in the vegetable stock and bring to the boil.
- Simmer for 20 minutes then stir in the crème fraiche and blend until smooth with a stick blender.
- Try the soup and adjust the seasoning with salt and pepper.
- Stir in the parsley then ladle into warm bowls.

### Tomato and Basil Soup

128

- Replace the parsley with a small bunch of roughly chopped basil.

129

**SERVES 4**

# Beetroot and Tomato Soup

- Heat the oil in a saucepan and fry the onion for 5 minutes or until softened. Add the garlic and cook for 2 more minutes then stir in the tomatoes and beetroot.
- Pour in the vegetable stock and bring to the boil.
- Simmer for 10 minutes then blend until smooth with a stick blender.
- Try the soup and adjust the seasoning with salt and pepper.
- Ladle into warm bowls and serve immediately.

PREPARATION TIME 5 MINUTES

COOKING TIME 20 MINUTES

### INGREDIENTS

2 tbsp olive oil
1 onion, finely chopped
2 cloves garlic, crushed
200 g / 7 oz / 1 cup canned tomatoes, chopped
250 g / 9 oz / 1 cup cooked beetroot, cubed
500 ml / 18 fl. oz / 2 cups vegetable stock
salt and pepper

### Beetroot, Tomato and Feta Soup

130

- Add 100 g / 3 ½ oz / ½ cup of feta cheese to the soup in small cubes just before serving.

131

**SERVES 4**

# Nettle Soup

- Heat the oil in a saucepan and fry the onion for 5 minutes or until softened. Add the garlic and cook for 2 more minutes then stir in the nettles.
- Pour in the vegetable stock and bring to the boil, then add salt and pepper to taste.
- Ladle into 4 warm bowls and serve immediately.

PREPARATION TIME 5 MINUTES

COOKING TIME 10 MINUTES

### INGREDIENTS

2 tbsp olive oil
1 onion, finely chopped
2 cloves garlic, crushed
150 g / 5 ½ oz / 5 cups stinging nettles, chopped
1 L / 1 pint 16 fl. oz / 4 cups vegetable stock
salt and pepper

### Watercress Soup

132

- Replace the nettles with an equal weight of watercress and blend with a stick blender before serving.

## 133

**SERVES 4**

# Carrot Soup with Beetroot Crisps

PREPARATION TIME 5 MINUTES

COOKING TIME 40 MINUTES

......................................................

### INGREDIENTS

2 tbsp olive oil
1 onion, finely chopped
400 g / 14 oz / 2 ¾ cup carrots, peeled
and chopped
2 cloves garlic, crushed
1 l / 1 pint 16 fl. oz / 4 cups vegetable
stock
2 tbsp crème fraiche
salt and pepper
25 g / 1 oz / 1 cup beetroot crisps

- Heat the oil in a saucepan and fry the onion and carrot for 10 minutes.
- Add the garlic and cook for 2 more minutes then pour in the vegetable stock and bring to the boil.
- Simmer for 25 minutes then stir in the crème fraiche and blend until smooth with a stick blender.
- Try the soup and adjust the seasoning with salt and pepper, then ladle into warm bowls.
- Crush some of the beetroot crisps and sprinkle on top, then garnish with a few whole crisps.

### Carrot and Coriander Soup  134

- Fry 1 tsp of crushed coriander (cilantro) seeds with the onions and stir in 2 tbsp chopped fresh coriander leaves after the soup has been pureed.

## 135

**SERVES 4**

# Provencal Pistou Soup

PREPARATION TIME 10 MINUTES

COOKING TIME 18 MINUTES

......................................................

### INGREDIENTS

2 tbsp olive oil
1 onion, finely chopped
2 cloves garlic, crushed
75 g / 2 ½ oz / ½ cup green beans
75 g / 2 ½ oz / ¾ cup mange tout,
chopped
75 g / 2 ½ oz / ½ cup celery hearts,
sliced
75 g / 2 ½ oz / ½ cup fresh peas
75 g / 2 ½ oz / ½ cup fresh broad
beans, podded weight
200 g / 7 oz / ½ cup canned butter
beans, drained
1 l / 1 pint 16 fl. oz / 4 cups vegetable
stock

FOR THE PISTOU
1 clove garlic, peeled
50 g / 1 ¾ oz / 1 ½ cups basil leaves,
chopped
4 tbsp olive oil

- Heat the oil in a saucepan and fry the onion for 5 minutes or until softened. Add the garlic and cook for 2 more minutes then stir in the vegetables and butter beans.
- Pour in the vegetable stock and bring to the boil.
- Turn down the heat and simmer for 10 minutes.
- Meanwhile, crush the garlic with a mortar and pestle, then add the basil and a pinch of salt and pound to a paste. Stir in the olive oil then divide the pistou between 4 small bowls.
- Try the soup and adjust the seasoning with salt and pepper.
- Ladle the soup into 4 warm bowls and serve each one with a portion of pistou for stirring in at the table.

### Tuna and Pistou Soup 136

- Omit the butterbeans and add 200 g / 7 oz / ¾ cups of cubed fresh tuna steak to the pan 2 minutes before the end of cooking time.

**137**

**SERVES 4**

# Bacon and Onion Gratin

## Mushroom and Onion Gratin

**138**

- Replace the bacon with 100 g / 3 ½ oz / ⅔ cup of sliced button mushrooms.

## Bacon and Leek Gratin

**139**

- Replace the onions with 2 thinly sliced leeks.

PREPARATION TIME 5 MINUTES

COOKING TIME 30 MINUTES

----

### INGREDIENTS

600 ml / 1 pint / 2 ½ cups whole milk
3 tbsp butter
1 tbsp plain (all purpose) flour
75 g / 2 ½ oz / ¾ cup Cheddar, grated
8 rashers of smoked bacon
1 large onion, halved and thinly sliced

- Preheat the oven to 190°C (170°C fan) / 375F / gas 5 and bring the milk to a simmer.
- Heat the butter in a small saucepan then stir in the flour and cook for 1 minute.
- Gradually incorporate the hot milk, stirring continuously to avoid any lumps forming.
- Continue to stir until it starts to bubble then stir in the cheese and season with salt and pepper.
- Arrange the bacon and onions in 4 small gratin dishes then spoon over the sauce.
- Cook the gratins in the oven for 20 minutes or until the onions are cooked.

**140**

SERVES 4

# Aubergine and Courgettes with Walnuts

PREPARATION TIME 5 MINUTES

COOKING TIME 30 MINUTES

### INGREDIENTS

4 tbsp olive oil
1 onion, finely chopped
1 aubergine (eggplant), finely chopped
2 courgettes (zucchini), finely chopped
1 clove garlic, crushed
100 g / 3 ½ oz / ¾ cup walnuts, chopped
2 tbsp flat leaf parsley, chopped
salt and pepper

- Heat the olive oil in a large sauté pan and fry the onion, aubergine and courgette with a pinch of salt for 25 minutes, stirring occasionally.
- When any liquid that comes out of the vegetables has evaporated and they start to turn golden, add the garlic and cook for 2 more minutes.
- Stir in the walnuts and parsley then season to taste with salt and pepper.

## Sautéed Aubergine with Pine Nuts

**141**

- Replace the walnuts with toasted pine nuts.

**142**

SERVES 4

# Courgettes Stuffed with Goats' Cheese

PREPARATION TIME 20 MINUTES

COOKING TIME 8 MINUTES

### INGREDIENTS

4 courgettes (zucchini)
150 g / 5 ½ oz / 1 cup fresh goats' cheese
1 tsp lemon zest, finely grated
2 tbsp chives, chopped

### TO SERVE

4 large tomatoes, diced
2 tbsp olive oil
½ lemon, juiced
basil leaves, to garnish

- Cut the ends off the courgettes and remove the middles with an apple corer.
- Mix the goats' cheese with the lemon zest and chives and plenty of black pepper, then pack it into the cavities.
- Steam the courgettes for 8 minutes or until tender, then slice and serve on a bed of tomatoes.
- Drizzle over the oil and lemon and garnish with basil.

## Courgettes Stuffed with Dolcelatte

**143**

- Replace the goats' cheese with an equal amount of Dolcelatte.

144

SERVES 4

# Carrots with Cumin and Paprika Butter

- Cook the carrots in boiling salted water for 12 minutes or until tender. Drain well.
- Meanwhile, beat the butter with the spices and a pinch of salt until smooth.
- Toss the carrots with the spiced butter and divide between 4 warm bowls.

PREPARATION TIME 5 MINUTES

COOKING TIME 12 MINUTES

......................................................

### INGREDIENTS

450 g / 1 lb / 3 cups carrots, sliced
50 g / 1 ¾ oz / ¼ cup butter, softened
1 tsp ground cumin
½ tsp smoked paprika

## Carrots with Coriander and Garlic Butter

145

- Substitute the cumin and paprika in the butter with 1 tsp of ground coriander and 1 tsp of crushed garlic.

146

SERVES 4

# Jacket Potatoes with Chilli Con Carne

- Preheat the oven to 220°C (200°C fan) / 430F / gas 7.
- Heat the oil in a large saucepan and fry the onion and pepper for 3 minutes. Add the garlic and Cayenne and cook for 2 minutes, then add the mince.
- Fry the mince until it starts to brown then add the chopped tomatoes, stock and kidney beans.
- Cook the chilli con carne for 30 minutes, stirring occasionally, until the mince is tender and the sauce has thickened a little.
- Meanwhile, prick the potatoes and microwave for 5 minutes. Transfer to the oven and bake for 25 minutes.
- Taste the chilli for seasoning and add salt and freshly ground black pepper as necessary.
- Cut the potatoes in half and spoon over the chilli then sprinkle with coriander.

PREPARATION TIME 5 MINUTES

COOKING TIME 40 MINUTES

......................................................

### INGREDIENTS

2 tbsp olive oil
1 red onion, chopped
1 red pepper, deseeded and chopped
2 cloves garlic, crushed
½ tsp Cayenne pepper
450 g / 1 lb / 2 cups minced beef
400 g / 14 oz / 2 cups canned tomatoes, chopped
200 ml / 7 fl. oz / ¾ cup beef stock
400 g / 14 oz / 4 cups canned kidney beans, drained
4 baking potatoes
salt and pepper
1 tbsp coriander (cilantro) leaves, chopped

## Chilli Con Carne in a Roll

147

- Try serving the chilli con carne in hollowed out bread rolls for an even quicker dinner.

148

SERVES 4

# Stuffed Courgettes

## Crispy Stuffed Courgettes

149

- Top the sausagemeat mixture with a layer of fresh breadcrumbs and drizzle with olive oil before baking for a crispy topping.

## Chorizo Stuffed Courgettes

150

- Replace the sausages with soft fresh cooking chorizo.

PREPARATION TIME 15 MINUTES

COOKING TIME 30 MINUTES

### INGREDIENTS

4 courgettes (zucchini)
6 good quality pork sausages, skinned
2 tbsp crème fraiche
1 tsp lemon zest, finely grated
2 tbsp flat leaf parsley, chopped

- Preheat the oven to 220°C (200°C fan) / 430F / gas 7.
- Cut the courgettes in half and use a melon baller to scoop out the middles.
- Mix the sausagemeat with the crème fraiche, lemon zest and parsley, then spoon it into the courgette cavities.
- Arrange the courgettes in a roasting tin and bake in the oven for 30 minutes or until golden brown and cooked through.

**151**

**SERVES 4**

# Boiled Potatoes with Garlic Mayonnaise

- Boil the potatoes in salted water for 12 minutes or until tender then drain well and arrange on a warm serving plate.
- Mix the mayonnaise with the garlic and lemon juice and spoon the mixture over the potatoes.
- Sprinkle over the parsley and serve.

PREPARATION TIME 15 MINUTES

COOKING TIME 40 MINUTES

### INGREDIENTS

800 g / 1 lb 12 oz / 4 ½ cup maris
piper potatoes, peeled and cubed
4 tbsp mayonnaise
1 clove garlic, crushed
1 tbsp lemon juice
2 tbsp flat leaf parsley, chopped

## Potatoes with Stilton Mayonnaise

**152**

- Omit the garlic and lemon juice and stir 75 g / 3 oz / ⅓ cup crumbled Stilton into the mayonnaise.

**153**

**SERVES 4**

# Tabbouleh

- Put the bulgur wheat in a bowl and pour over enough boiling water to just cover it. Cover the bowl tightly and leave to soak for 15 minutes.
- Tip the bulgur wheat into a sieve and run it under the cold tap to cool. Drain well.
- Stir the parsley, tomato and shallot into the bulgur and dress with the lemon juice and olive oil.
- Taste for seasoning and adjust with sea salt and black pepper.

PREPARATION TIME 20 MINUTES

### INGREDIENTS

150 g / 5 ½ oz / ⅔ cup bulgur wheat
a small bunch flat leaf parsley, finely
chopped
2 tomatoes, deseeded and finely
chopped
2 shallots, finely chopped
1 lemon, juiced
2 tbsp extra virgin olive oil
salt and pepper

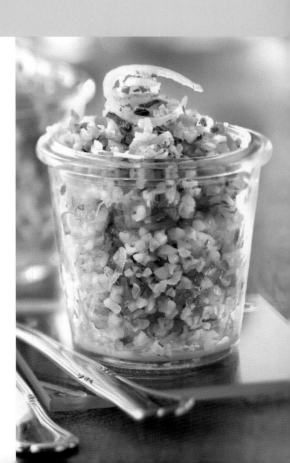

## Middle Eastern Tabbouleh

**154**

- For a more traditional Tabbouleh, halve the amount of bulgur wheat and double the amount of finely chopped parsley.

**155**

**SERVES 4**

# Roasted Vegetable Tapenade

PREPARATION TIME 10 MINUTES

COOKING TIME 25 MINUTES

### INGREDIENTS

1 courgette (zucchini), cubed
1 aubergine (eggplant), cubed
1 red pepper, deseeded and cubed
1 yellow pepper, deseeded and cubed
4 tbsp olive oil
salt and pepper
50 g / 1 ¾ oz / ⅓ cup mixed olives, pitted
1 tbsp capers
toasted bread to serve

- Preheat the oven to 180°C (160°C fan) / 355F / gas 4.
- Toss the vegetables with half of the oil and season with salt and pepper then roast for 25 minutes.
- Tip the vegetables into a food processor and add the olives, capers and the rest of the oil.
- Pulse until finely chopped and well mixed then spoon into a bowl.
- Serve with toasted bread to spoon it on to.

## Pickled Vegetable Tapenade

**156**

- Replace the roasted vegetables with 100 g / 3 ½ oz / ½ cup pickled beetroot slices and 100 g / 3 ½ oz / ½ cup of sweet dill pickles.

**157**

**SERVES 4**

# French Onion Soup

PREPARATION TIME 5 MINUTES

COOKING TIME 40 MINUTES

### INGREDIENTS

2 tbsp olive oil
3 onions, sliced
2 cloves garlic, crushed
1 l / 1 pint 16 fl. oz / 4 cups vegetable stock
salt and pepper

### FOR THE CROUTES

1 baguette, sliced
100 g / 3 ½ oz / 1 cup Gruyere, grated

- Heat the oil in a saucepan and fry the onions for 20 minutes. Add the garlic and cook for 2 more minutes then stir in the vegetable stock and bring to the boil.
- Simmer for 15 minutes then taste the soup and adjust the seasoning with salt and pepper.
- Meanwhile, preheat the grill to its highest setting.
- Toast the baguette slices on one side under the grill then turn them over and sprinkle with cheese.
- Grill the other side until the cheese is golden and bubbling.
- Ladle the soup into 4 warm bowls and float the croutes on top.

## Beer and Onion Soup

**158**

- Replace 300 ml / ½ pt / 1 ¼ cups of the vegetable stock with 300 ml / ½ pt / 1 ¼ cups of beer and spread the baguette slices with grain mustard. Top with the cheese.

## MAKES 20-24 | 159 Goats' Cheese Samosas

- Preheat the oven to 180°C (160°C fan) / 355F / gas 4 and grease a large baking tray.
- Mash the goats' cheese with the garlic, lemon zest and parsley and season with salt and pepper.
- Cut the pile of filo sheets in half then take one halved sheet and brush it with melted butter.
- Arrange a heaped teaspoon of goat's cheese at one end then fold the corner across and triangle-fold it into a samosa shape.
- Transfer the samosa to the baking tray and repeat with the rest of the filo and goats' cheese.
- Bake the samosas for 12–15 minutes or until the filo is crisp and golden brown.
- Serve on a bed of spinach.

PREPARATION TIME 25 MINUTES

COOKING TIME 12–15 MINUTES

### INGREDIENTS

200 g / 7 oz / 1 ¼ cup fresh goats' cheese
1 clove garlic, crushed
1 lemon, zest finely grated
2 tbsp flat leaf parsley, chopped
salt and pepper
225 g / 8 oz filo pastry
100 g / 3 ½ oz / ½ cup butter, melted
baby leaf spinach, to serve

### Goats' Cheese and Walnut Samosas | 160

- Add 50 g / 2 oz / ½ cup of chopped walnuts to the goats' cheese mixture.

## SERVES 4 | 161 Deep-fried Fish Balls

- Put the fish, spring onions, garlic, olives and spices in a food processor with a big pinch of salt and whizz to a sticky paste.
- Heat the oil in a deep fat fryer, according to the manufacturer's instructions, to a temperature of 180°C.
- Use an ice cream scoop to portion the mixture into balls and drop them straight into the hot oil.
- Fry the fish balls for 3–4 minutes, turning once, or until they are golden brown.
- Line a large bowl with a thick layer of kitchen paper and when they are ready, tip them into the bowl to remove any excess oil.
- Sprinkle with a little sea salt to taste and serve immediately on a bed of lettuce with lemon wedges.

PREPARATION TIME 15 MINUTES

COOKING TIME 3-4 MINUTES

### INGREDIENTS

400 g / 14 oz / 2 cups white fish fillets
4 spring onions (scallions), chopped
1 clove garlic, crushed
50 g / 1 ¾ oz / ⅓ cup black olives, pitted
1 tsp ground cumin
½ tsp ground coriander (cilantro)
½ tsp ground cinnamon
2–3 litres / 3 ½ pints–5 pints / 8–12 cups sunflower oil
lettuce leaves and lemon wedges, to serve

### Thai Fish Balls | 162

- Replace the olives and spices with 1 tbsp of Thai red curry paste.

**163**

**SERVES 4**

# Potatoes Stuffed with Bacon and Cheese

### Three-cheese Potatoes

**164**

- Stir 100 g / 3 ½ oz / ½ oz cup of Roquefort into 150 g / 5 oz / ⅔ cup of Mascarpone and spoon it into the potatoes. instead of the bacon and crème fraiche.

### Potatoes Stuffed with Tuna and Cheese

**165**

- Replace the bacon with 150 g / 5 oz / ½ cup of canned tuna.

PREPARATION TIME 10 MINUTES

COOKING TIME 25 MINUTES

.............................................

### INGREDIENTS

4 medium baking potatoes
150 g / 5 ½ oz / ⅔ cup streaky bacon, chopped
1 tbsp olive oil
2 tbsp crème fraiche
2 tbsp chives, chopped
4 slices Raclette cheese

- Preheat the oven to 220⁰C (200⁰C fan) / 430F / gas 7.
- Prick the potatoes and cook them in a microwave on high for 5 minutes.
- Meanwhile, fry the bacon in the oil for 4 minutes then stir in the crème fraiche and chives.
- Cut a slice off the top of the potatoes and scoop out the centres with a teaspoon.
- Mix 4 tablespoon of the scooped out potato with the bacon mixture, then stuff it back into the potato shells.
- Lay a slice of Raclette over each potato then bake in the oven for 20 minutes or until golden brown.

**166**

**SERVES 4**

# Prawn Cocktail in Courgette Cups

- Use a sharp paring knife to cut the tops off the courgettes in a zigzag pattern. Scoop out the centres with a teaspoon and discard.
- Mix the mayonnaise with the ketchup, paprika and lemon juice then stir in the prawns.
- Taste for seasoning and add salt and pepper as necessary.
- Spoon the prawn cocktail into the courgette cups and put the lids back on.
- Sprinkle with chopped oregano.

**PREPARATION TIME 10 MINUTES**

## INGREDIENTS

4 round courgettes (zucchini)
200 g / 7 oz / ⅔ cup mayonnaise
2 tbsp tomato ketchup
½ tsp smoked paprika
1 tbsp lemon juice
200 g / 7 oz / 2 cups / ¾ cup cooked prawns (shrimps), peeled
salt and pepper
2 tbsp oregano, chopped

### Tuna Mayonnaise in Courgette Cups

**167**

- Omit the tomato ketchup and replace the prawns with canned tuna.

**168**

**SERVES 6**

# Gazpacho Soup

- Put all of the ingredients in a liquidiser with a big pinch of salt and freshly ground black pepper and blend until smooth.
- Pass the soup through a sieve, then taste for seasoning and add more salt and pepper if necessary.
- Ladle the soup into bowls and garnish with chive flowers. Serve with small bowls of cubed vegetables that can be added to the soup like croutons.

**PREPARATION TIME 10 MINUTES**

## INGREDIENTS

1 cucumber, peeled and chopped
4 large, ripe tomatoes, chopped
1 red pepper, deseeded and chopped
½ clove of garlic, crushed
2 spring onions (scallions), finely chopped
1 tbsp sherry vinegar
100 ml / 3 ½ fl. oz / ½ cup extra virgin olive oil
salt and pepper

### TO SERVE
small cubes of onion, peppers, tomato and cucumber
chive flowers, to garnish

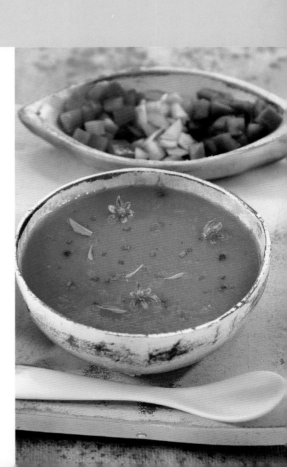

### Spicy Gazpacho Soup

**169**

- Add 1 finely chopped green pepper and a few drops of hot sauce to the vegetables before blending.

53

**170**

SERVES 4

# Mixed Vegetable Tortilla

PREPARATION TIME 10 MINUTES

COOKING TIME 20 MINUTES

### INGREDIENTS

4 tbsp olive oil
1 red onion, thinly sliced
1 red pepper, deseeded and finely chopped
3 boiled potatoes, cooled and cubed
75 g / 2 ½ oz / ½ cup frozen peas, defrosted
6 eggs
salt and pepper

- Heat half the oil in a non-stick frying pan and fry the onion and peppers for 5 minutes.
- Meanwhile, gently beat the eggs in a jug to break up the yolks. When the onions are ready, stir them into the eggs with the potatoes and peas and season with salt and pepper.
- Heat the rest of the oil in the frying pan then pour in the egg mixture.
- Cook over a gentle heat for 6–8 minutes or until the egg has set round the outside, but the centre is still a bit runny.
- Turn it out onto a plate, then slide it back into the pan and cook the other side for 4–6 minutes.
- Leave to cool for 5 minutes then cut into wedges and serve.

## Vegetable and Anchovy Tortilla  **171**

- Finely chop 6 anchovy fillets in oil and add them to the vegetables. Leave out the salt when seasoning to balance the salty anchovies.

**172**

SERVES 4

# Tortilla Espanol

PREPARATION TIME 10 MINUTES

COOKING TIME 20 MINUTES

### INGREDIENTS

4 tbsp olive oil
1 onion, thinly sliced
4 boiled potatoes, cooled and cubed
6 eggs
salt and pepper

- Heat half the oil in a non-stick frying pan and fry the onion with a pinch of salt and pepper for 5 minutes.
- Meanwhile, gently beat the eggs in a jug to break up the yolks. When the onions are ready, stir them into the eggs with the potatoes and season with salt and pepper.
- Heat the rest of the oil in the frying pan then pour in the egg mixture.
- Cook over a gentle heat for 6–8 minutes or until the egg has set round the outside, but the centre is still a bit runny.
- Turn it out onto a plate, then slide it back into the pan and cook the other side for 4–6 minutes.
- Leave to cool for 5 minutes then cut into wedges and serve.

## Potato and Chorizo Tortilla   **173**

- Slice 150 g / 5 oz / ¾ cup of chorizo and add it to the onions when you fry them.

174

**SERVES 4**

# Baked New Potatoes

### Baked Jerusalem Artichokes

175

- Replace the potatoes with an equal quantity of Jerusalem artichokes.

### Baked New Potatoes with Garlic

176

- Break a bulb of garlic into individual cloves and add them to the foil parcel.

PREPARATION TIME 5 MINUTES

COOKING TIME 40 MINUTES

............................................................

### INGREDIENTS

8 medium new potatoes
2 tbsp olive oil
sea salt
2 sprigs rosemary

- Preheat the oven to 220⁰C (200⁰C fan) / 430F / gas 7.
- Prick the potatoes and cook them in a microwave on high for 5 minutes.
- Put the potatoes in the centre of a large sheet of foil, drizzle with olive oil and sprinkle with sea salt flakes.
- Add the rosemary sprigs, then fold up the foil and scrunch to seal.
- Bake the potato parcel in the oven for 35 minutes or until cooked through.

# Mediterranean Vegetable Salad

## Mediterranean Steak Salad

178

- Griddle a large sirloin steak for 3 minutes on each side then cut into thin slices and toss with the rest of the salad ingredients.

## Mediterranean Snapper Salad

179

- Brush 12 red snapper fillets with olive oil and cook on a hot griddle for 2 minutes on each side, then toss with the rest of the salad ingredients.

**PREPARATION TIME 8 MINUTES**

### INGREDIENTS

2 courgettes (zucchini), cut into batons
1 jar preserved artichokes in oil, drained
1 jar mixed roasted peppers in oil, drained, oil reserved
8 cherry tomatoes, quartered
50 g / 1 ¾ oz / ⅓ cup kalamata olives, pitted
50 g / 1 ¾ oz / 1 cup rocket (arugula) leaves

### FOR THE DRESSING
2 tbsp oil from the pepper jar
½ lemon, juiced
salt and pepper

- Toss all of the vegetables, tomatoes, olives and rocket together and divide between 4 plates.
- Whisk the pepper oil with the lemon juice and season to taste then spoon it over the salad.

**180**

**SERVES 4**

# Mustard Chicken with Spinach and Feta

- Preheat the grill to its highest setting.
- Mix together the mustard, oil and rosemary with a pinch of salt and pepper and rub it over the chicken breasts.
- Grill the chicken for 5 minutes on each side or until cooked through.
- Meanwhile, toss together the spinach, onion, feta and pine nuts and divide between 4 plates.
- Put the dressing ingredients in a jar and shake to emulsify, then put the jar on the table so people can help themselves.
- Serve the chicken alongside the salad on the plates.

PREPARATION TIME 10 MINUTES

COOKING TIME 10 MINUTES

**INGREDIENTS**

2 tbsp grain mustard
1 tbsp olive oil
1 tsp rosemary, finely chopped
salt and pepper
4 chicken breasts

FOR THE SALAD
75 g / 2 ½ oz / 1 cup baby spinach leaves
1 small red onion, sliced
100 g / 3 ½ oz / ⅔ cup feta, cubed
30 g / 1 oz pine nuts

FOR THE DRESSING
1 tsp runny honey
1 tsp wholegrain mustard
2 tbsp white wine vinegar
4 tbsp olive oil

## Peppered Mackerel Salad

**181**

- When you're really short of time, omit the chicken and flake 2 peppered smoked mackerel fillets over the salad instead.

**182**

**SERVES 2**

# Tomatoes and Broccoli Conchiglie

- Preheat the oven to 220°C (200°C fan) / 430F / gas 7.
- Coat the broccoli, tomatoes and garlic with oil and spread them out in a roasting tin. Roast for 15 minutes or until the tomatoes are starting to burst and the broccoli is tender.
- Meanwhile, cook the conchiglie in boiling salted water according to the packet instructions or until al dente.
- Reserve a ladle of pasta water and drain the rest.
- Stir the pasta into the roasting tin with the reserved cooking water and the capers and stir to coat in the juices.
- Divide between 2 warm bowls and serve.

PREPARATION TIME 4 MINUTES

COOKING TIME 15 MINUTES

**INGREDIENTS**

100 g / 3 ½ oz / 1 cup broccoli, broken into small florets
100 g / 3 ½ oz / ⅔ cup cherry tomatoes
1 clove garlic, halved
4 tbsp olive oil
200 g / 7 oz / 2 ⅔ cup conchiglie pasta
2 tbsp baby capers

## Conchiglie with Broccoli and Anchovies

**183**

- Omit the tomatoes and stir 6 finely chopped anchovy fillets into the pasta when you add the capers.

**SERVES 4**

# Celery, Cambozola and Cashew Salad

PREPARATION TIME 5 MINUTES

## INGREDIENTS

50 g / 1 ¾ oz / ⅓ cup cashew nuts
8 celery sticks, cut into 8 cm (3 in)
lengths
150 g / 5 ½ oz / 1 ½ cup Cambozola,
sliced
8 cherry tomatoes, quartered
4 tbsp olive oil
salt and pepper

- Chop half of the cashews and leave the rest whole. Mix them with the celery, Cambozola and tomatoes and divide between 4 bowls.
- Drizzle with olive oil and sprinkle with salt and pepper before serving.

185

**SERVES 4**

# Cucumber, Radish and Baby Corn Salad

PREPARATION TIME 10 MINUTES

## INGREDIENTS

1 cucumber, thinly sliced
a small bunch of mint, leaves only
150 g / 5 ½ oz / 1 ½ cup radishes,
thinly sliced
100 g / 3 ½ oz / 1 cup baby sweetcorn,
thinly sliced

FOR THE DRESSING
1 tsp white miso soup paste
1 tsp caster (superfine) sugar
1 tbsp rice wine vinegar

- First make the dressing. Mix the miso soup paste with 4 tbsp boiling water and stir in the sugar and vinegar to dissolve. Leave to cool.
- Mix the cucumber with the mint, radish and baby corn slices and drizzle over the dressing.

186

SERVES 4

# Preserved Artichoke and Onion Salad

- Mix all of the ingredients together in a bowl and sprinkle with salt and pepper.
- Leave for 30 minutes for the flavours to infuse then divide between 4 plates and serve.

**PREPARATION TIME 30 MINUTES**

## INGREDIENTS

400 g / 14 oz / 2 ⅔ cup canned
artichoke hearts in water, drained
100 g / 3 ½ oz / ⅔ cup pickled
silverskin onions
100 g / 3 ½ oz / ⅔ cup cherry
tomatoes, quartered
1 tbsp chives, chopped
4 tbsp extra virgin olive oil
a few sprigs curly parsley
salt and pepper

# Vietnamese Prawn Salad

187

SERVES 4

**PREPARATION TIME 10 MINUTES**

## INGREDIENTS

12 cooked king prawns (shrimps),
peeled leaving tails intact
½ cucumber, julienned
½ red pepper, julienned
4 spring onions (scallions), sliced
¼ Chinese cabbage, shredded

### FOR THE DRESSING
1 tbsp caster (superfine) sugar
1 tbsp fish sauce
1 lime, juiced
1 clove garlic, crushed
1 red chilli (chili), finely chopped

- To make the dressing, stir the caster sugar into the fish sauce and lime juice to dissolve, then stir in the garlic and chilli.
- Mix the cucumber, peppers, spring onion and cabbage together and divide between 4 bowls.
- Arrange the prawns on top then spoon over the dressing.

# Aubergine and Oyster Sauce

188

SERVES 4

**PREPARATION TIME 5 MINUTES**

**COOKING TIME 12 MINUTES**

## INGREDIENTS

4 tbsp vegetable oil
2 aubergines (eggplant), cubed
3 tbsp oyster sauce
1 tbsp sweet chilli sauce
2 spring onions (scallions), quartered
and cut into short lengths
coriander (cilantro), to garnish

- Heat the oil in a large wok and stir-fry the aubergine for 5 minutes or until golden.
- Add the oyster sauce, chilli sauce and 2 tablespoons of water to the pan and cook for another 5 minutes or until almost all of the sauce has been absorbed.
- Add the spring onions and stir-fry for 1 more minute then garnish with coriander and serve.

189

SERVES 4

# Watermelon, Feta and Basil Salad

PREPARATION TIME 5 MINUTES

### INGREDIENTS

½ small watermelon, deseeded and cut into chunks
100 g / 3 ½ oz / ⅔ cup feta, cubed
4 tbsp basil leaves, shredded
4 tbsp extra virgin olive oil
sea salt

• Mix the watermelon with the feta and divide between 4 plates.
• Scatter over the basil and drizzle with olive oil then sprinkle with sea salt.

### Watermelon, Feta and Mint Salad

190

• Replace the basil with shredded fresh mint leaves and squeeze over the juice of half a lemon at the end.

191

SERVES 4

# Smoked Mackerel and Olive Salad

PREPARATION TIME 5 MINUTES

### INGREDIENTS

4 smoked mackerel fillets
8 spring onions (scallions), sliced lengthways
50 g / 1 ¾ oz / ⅓ cup green olives
50 g / 1 ¾ oz / ⅓ cup black olives
1 orange, juiced
2 tbsp olive oil
salt

• Arrange the mackerel, onions and olives on 4 plates.
• Whisk the orange juice and oil together with a pinch of salt then drizzle it over the salad.

### Smoked Mackerel and Fennel Salad

192

• Replace half the spring onions with a sliced fennel bulb and substitute the olives with 2 tbsp of capers.

**193**

**SERVES 4**

# Asparagus with Dolcelatte Cream

## Asparagus with Mustard Cream

 194

- Replace the Dolcelatte with 1 tbsp Dijon mustard.

## Asparagus with Lemon Cream

195

- Omit the Dolcelatte and stir the zest and juice of a lemon into the hot cream just before serving.

PREPARATION TIME 10 MINUTES

COOKING TIME 4–5 MINUTES

### INGREDIENTS

400 g / 14 oz / 4 cups fresh asparagus
100 g / 3 ½ oz / 1 cup Dolcelatte, cubed
300 ml / 10 ½ fl. oz / 1 ½ cup double (heavy) cream
pepper

- Snap the woody ends off the asparagus and cut the spears in half. Steam the asparagus for 5 minutes or until tender.
- Meanwhile, put the Dolcelatte in a small saucepan with the cream and some freshly ground black pepper.
- Bring to a gentle simmer, stirring constantly, then take off the heat.
- Divide the asparagus between 4 warm plates and spoon over the sauce.

## 196

**SERVES 6**

# Chilled Cucumber and Mint Soup

**PREPARATION TIME 5 MINUTES**

### INGREDIENTS

2 cucumbers, peeled and chopped
½ clove garlic, crushed
a small bunch mint, chopped
500 ml / 18 fl. oz / 2 cups vegetable stock
salt and pepper
100 g / 3 ½ oz / 1 cup feta, cubed

- Put the cucumber, garlic, mint and vegetable stock in a liquidiser and blend until smooth.
- Taste the soup and adjust the seasoning with salt and black pepper.
- Chill the soup in the fridge until you are ready to serve, then ladle into small bowls and garnish with feta cubes.

## 197

**SERVES 4**

# Baked Potatoes Stuffed with Sausage Meat

**PREPARATION TIME 10 MINUTES**

**COOKING TIME 40 MINUTES**

### INGREDIENTS

4 medium baking potatoes
8 good quality pork sausages, skinned
1 tbsp wholegrain mustard
1 clove garlic, crushed

- Preheat the oven to 220°C (200°C fan) / 430F / gas 7.
- Prick the potatoes and cook them in a microwave on high for 5 minutes.
- Cut a slice off the top of the potatoes and scoop out the centres into a bowl.
- Mix it with the sausagemeat, mustard and garlic, then stuff it back into the potato shells.
- Turn the sliced-off sections cut side up and put them on top of the stuffing.
- Bake in the oven for 35 minutes or until golden brown and cooked through.

**198**

**SERVES 4**

# Onion Bhajis

- Heat the oil in a deep fat fryer, according to the manufacturer's instructions, to a temperature of 180°C.
- Mix the flour with the lime zest, spices and a big pinch of salt.
- Make a well in the centre and break in the eggs, then incorporate all the flour from round the outside with a whisk.
- Stir the onions into the batter then use an ice cream scoop to portion the mixture into bhajis, dropping them straight into the hot oil, 4 at a time.
- Fry the bhajis for 1–2 minutes, turning halfway through, until they are crisp and golden brown.
- Transfer the bhajis to a kitchen paper lined bowl and continue with the rest of the batter.
- Sprinkle with a little sea salt to taste and serve immediately.

PREPARATION TIME 10 MINUTES

COOKING TIME 10 MINUTES

## INGREDIENTS

110 g / 4 oz / ⅔ cup plain (all purpose) flour
1 lime, zest finely grated
½ tsp cumin seeds, crushed
½ tsp coriander (cilantro) seeds, crushed
2 large eggs
3 red onions, halved and thinly sliced
2–3 litres / 3 ½–5 pints / 8–12 cups sunflower oil
salt

# Spicy Baby New Potatoes

**199**

**SERVES 4**

PREPARATION TIME 8 MINUTES

COOKING TIME 45 MINUTES

## INGREDIENTS

800 g / 1 lb 12 oz / 4 ½ cups baby new potatoes
1 tsp mustard seeds
1 tsp coriander (cilantro) seeds

½ tsp ground cumin
½ tsp ground cinnamon
4 tbsp olive oil
coriander (cilantro) leaves, to garnish

- Preheat the oven to 200°C (180°C fan) / 390F / gas 6.
- Boil the potatoes in salted water for 10 minutes then drain well and leave to steam dry for 2 minutes.
- Put the oil in a large roasting tin in the oven to heat for 2 minutes.
- Toss the potatoes with the spices and plenty of salt and pepper, then add them to the roasting tin and stir to coat in the oil.
- Roast the potatoes for 30 minutes or until golden brown then garnish with coriander leaves.

# Red Curry Potatoes

**200**

**SERVES 4**

PREPARATION TIME 5 MINUTES

COOKING TIME 40 MINUTES

coriander (cilantro) leaves
strips of green chilli (chili), to garnish

## INGREDIENTS

800 g / 1 lb 12 oz / 4 ½ cups maris piper potatoes, peeled and cubed
2 tbsp Thai red curry paste
1 tsp mustard seeds

- Preheat the oven to 220°C (200°C fan) / 430F / gas 7 and put a large roasting tin in to heat.
- Boil the potatoes in salted water for 8 minutes then drain well and leave to steam dry for 2 minutes.
- Mix the curry paste and mustard seeds together then brush it over the potatoes.
- Put the potatoes into the hot roasting tin and roast for 30 minutes or until golden and toasted at the edges, turning occasionally.
- Garnish with coriander leaves and green chilli just before serving.

# MAINS

201

SERVES 2

# Griddled Salmon with Summer Vegetables

PREPARATION TIME 10 MINUTES

COOKING TIME 12 MINUTES

........................................................

### INGREDIENTS

75 g / 2 ½ oz / ½ cup French beans
75 g / 2 ½ oz / ½ cup fresh peas
1 courgette (zucchini)
2 portions salmon fillet, skinned
3 tbsp olive oil
salt and pepper
75 g / 2 ½ oz / ¾ cup mange tout
1 tbsp garden mint, chopped
1 tbsp flat leaf parsley, chopped
½ lemon, juiced

- Blanch the French beans and peas for 4 minutes then drain and refresh in cold water.
- Use a vegetable peeler to shave the courgette into long ribbons.
- Heat a griddle pan until smoking hot on the stove.
- Brush the salmon fillets with 1 tablespoon of the oil and season with salt and pepper.
- Griddle the salmon for 2 minutes on each side.
- Meanwhile, heat the rest of the oil in a large sauté pan and add the beans, peas, courgette ribbons and mange tout.
- Stir-fry the vegetables for 4 minutes then sprinkle over the herbs and a squeeze of lemon juice.
- Spoon the vegetables into a warm serving dish. Turn the salmon fillets in any lemony juices left in the sauté pan before arranging them on top of the vegetables.

### Griddled Sword Fish with Summer Vegetables

202

- Replace the salmon with sword fish steaks.

203

SERVES 2

# Sesame-crusted Salmon with Soy Carrots

PREPARATION TIME 10 MINUTES

COOKING TIME 8–10 MINUTES

........................................................

### INGREDIENTS

1 egg white, beaten
1 tbsp cornflour (cornstarch)
2 portions salmon fillet, skinned
50 g / 1 ¾ oz / ¼ cup sesame seeds
4 tbsp olive oil
1 clove garlic, crushed
2 large carrots, julienned
2 tbsp soy sauce

- Mix the egg white with the cornflour and brush a thin layer onto the skinned side of the salmon. Dip the salmon in the sesame seeds, pressing down firmly so they stick in an even layer.
- Heat half the oil in a large frying pan and cook the salmon, sesame side down, for 4 minutes.
- Meanwhile, heat the rest of the oil in a sauté pan and fry the garlic and carrots for 3 minutes. Add the soy sauce and 2 tablespoons of water then put a lid on the pan and cook for 2 more minutes.
- Turn the salmon over, turn off the heat and let the other side cook in the residual heat of the pan for 2 minutes.
- Spoon the carrots on to 2 warm dinner plates and top with the salmon fillets.

### Sesame-crusted Sea Bass

204

- Replace the salmon with 2 portions cut from a large sea bass fillet.

205

**SERVES 4**

# Tuna Tortilla Wraps

- Fry the onion and chilli in the oil for 5 minutes or until starting to caramelise then add the tuna, sweetcorn, kidney beans and coriander. Cook for 3 minutes or until piping hot.
- Divide the tuna mixture between the tortillas and top with lettuce and tomato.

PREPARATION TIME 5 MINUTES

COOKING TIME 8 MINUTES

### INGREDIENTS

1 onion, finely chopped
1 red chilli (chili), finely chopped
2 tbsp olive oil
200 g / 7 oz / ¾ cup canned tuna, drained
100 g / 3 ½ oz / ½ cup canned sweetcorn, drained
100 g / 3 ½ oz / 1 cup canned kidney beans, drained
2 tbsp coriander (cilantro) leaves, chopped

### TO SERVE

4 flour tortillas
¼ iceberg lettuce, shredded
2 tomatoes, diced

### Tuna Wraps with Guacamole

206

- Cube an avocado and put it in a food processor with 2 spring onions, 1 chopped red chilli and the juice of a lime and blend. Spoon on top of the tuna mixture instead of the salad.

207

**SERVES 2**

# Tagliatelle with Pear and Roquefort

- Cook the tagliatelle in boiling salted water according to the packet instructions or until al dente.
- While the pasta is cooking, use a vegetable peeler to shave the pears into thin slices.
- When the pasta is ready, drain it well and toss with the olive oil then arrange it on 2 hot serving plates with the pear, Roquefort, walnuts and peppercorns.

PREPARATION TIME 5 MINUTES

COOKING TIME 12 MINUTES

### INGREDIENTS

200 g / 7 oz / 2 cups tagliatelle
1 ripe pear, quartered and cored
2 tbsp olive oil
100 g / 3 ½ oz / 1 cup Roquefort, cubed
1 tbsp walnuts, chopped
1 tsp pink peppercorns, crushed

### Pear and Roquefort Salad

208

- Omit the tagliatelle and use the pear, Roquefort and walnuts to dress a spinach and rocket salad.

## 209
**SERVES 4**

# Pork and Broccoli with Mustard Sauce

PREPARATION TIME 2 MINUTES

COOKING TIME 20 MINUTES

.....................................................................

### INGREDIENTS

2 tbsp olive oil
1 large onion, halved and sliced
2 garlic cloves, crushed
450 g / 1 lb / 3 cups pork fillet, thinly sliced
2 tsp Dijon mustard
1 tsp grain mustard
100 ml / 3 ½ fl. oz / ½ cup white wine
1 small head broccoli, broken into florets
400 ml / 14 fl. oz / 1 ⅔ cup double (heavy) cream
½ lemon, juiced
salt and pepper

- Heat the oil in a large sauté pan and fry the onion for 5 minutes. Add the garlic and cook for 2 more minutes then add the pork to the pan.
- Stir-fry the pork for 2 minutes until it starts to colour, then stir in the mustards and the wine.
- When the sauce starts to bubble, add the broccoli and stir to coat in the juices.
- Pour in the double cream and bring to a gentle simmer, then put the lid on and cook for 4 minutes.
- Stir the lemon juice into the sauce and season with salt and pepper just before serving.

### Pork and Broccoli with Ginger Sauce
## 210

- Omit the mustards and add 1 tbsp of thinly sliced root ginger to the onions when you fry them.

## 211
**SERVES 4**

# Guacamole Tacos

PREPARATION TIME 4 MINUTES

.....................................................................

### INGREDIENTS

4 ripe avocados
1 red onion, finely chopped
1 red chilli (chili), finely chopped
3 medium tomatoes, diced
2 tbsp coriander (cilantro) leaves, chopped
2 limes, juiced
chopped tomato and flat leaf parsley sprigs, to garnish

### TO SERVE
8 corn tacos

- Mash the avocados with a fork then stir in the rest of the guacamole ingredients. Season to taste with salt and white pepper.
- Divide the guacamole between 8 tacos and serve 2 tacos per person, garnished with extra tomato and parsley sprigs.

### Guacamole and Chorizo Tacos
## 212

- Fry 150 g / 5 oz / ¾ cup of sliced chorizo in 2 tbsp of olive oil then spoon it on top of the guacamole.

**213**

**SERVES 4**

# Beef and Parsley Burgers

## Beef and Basil Burgers

**214**

- Replace the parsley with basil and replace the mustard with 2 tsp of pesto.

## Boar and Parsley Burgers

**215**

- Replace the minced beef with an equal weight of minced wild boar.

PREPARATION TIME 10 MINUTES

COOKING TIME 10–12 MINUTES

### INGREDIENTS

450 g / 1 lb / 2 cups minced beef
2 salad onions, finely chopped
4 tbsp flat leaf parsley, chopped
1 tbsp baby capers
1 tsp Dijon mustard
2 tbsp olive oil

TO SERVE
baby salad leaves
4 salad onions, halved
4 sprigs flat leaf parsley

- Put the mince in a bowl with the onion, parsley, capers and mustard, and knead with your hands until well mixed and starting to get sticky.
- Divide the mixture into 4 and shape it into burgers, squeezing the patties firmly with your hands.
- Heat the oil in a large frying pan and cook the burgers for 10–12 minutes, turning every 2 minutes.
- Serve the burgers on a bed of salad leaves, garnished with salad onions and parsley.

**216**

**SERVES 2**

# Poached Egg and Bacon Rolls

## Poached Egg and Sausage Baps

**217**

- Fry 4 pork sausages over a low heat for 15 minutes, turning occasionally, and use in place of the bacon.

## BLT Baps

**218**

- Omit the poached eggs for a classic bacon, lettuce and tomato bap.

PREPARATION TIME 10 MINUTES

COOKING TIME 8 MINUTES

### INGREDIENTS

4 thick rashers streaky bacon
2 eggs
2 sesame rolls
2 lettuce leaves
1 large tomato, sliced
roasted new potatoes and extra salad to serve

- Preheat the grill to its highest setting and bring a wide saucepan of water to a gentle simmer.
- Grill the bacon for 2 minutes on each side or until crisp and golden brown.
- Meanwhile, crack each egg into a cup and pour them smoothly into the water, one at a time.
- Simmer gently for 3 minutes.
- Cut the rolls in half and add a lettuce leaf and a thick slice of tomato to the bottom halves.
- Top the tomato with the bacon. Use a slotted spoon to take the eggs out of the water and blot the underneath on a piece of kitchen paper before laying them on top of the bacon.
- Put the lids on the rolls and hold everything together with a wooden skewer.
- Serve with roasted new potatoes and extra salad.

# Cheese and Red Onion Burgers

**219**

**SERVES 2**

- Preheat the grill to its highest setting.
- Put the burgers and onion slices on a grill tray and brush with olive oil. Grill for 4 minutes on each side or until the burgers are cooked to your liking and the onions are caramelised at the edges.
- Cut the baps in half and add a lettuce leaf and the tomato slices to the bottom halves.
- Top the tomato with the burgers and lay the cheese on top, followed by the onions.
- Put the lids on the baps and serve.

PREPARATION TIME 5 MINUTES

COOKING TIME 8 MINUTES

### INGREDIENTS

2 beef burgers
1 red onion, peeled and sliced
2 tbsp olive oil
2 white baps
2 lettuce leaves
1 large tomato, sliced
4 slices mild Cheddar

### Stilton and Red Onion Burgers

**220**

- Replace the Cheddar with crumbled Stilton.

# Farfalle with Pepper and Basil Sauce

**221**

**SERVES 4**

- Cook the farfalle in boiling salted water according to the packet instructions or until al dente.
- While the pasta is cooking, heat the olive oil in a large frying pan and cook the garlic and peppers for 8 minutes, stirring occasionally.
- Scrape the mixture into a food processor and blend to a smooth puree, then return it to the frying pan.
- Drain the pasta and stir it into the pepper puree. Add the basil leaves and put the pan back over the heat for 1 minute to warm through before serving.

PREPARATION TIME 5 MINUTES

COOKING TIME 12 MINUTES

### INGREDIENTS

400 g / 14 oz / 2 cups farfalle pasta
4 tbsp olive oil
4 cloves garlic, crushed
2 orange peppers, finely chopped
a small bunch of basil, leaves only

### Farfalle with Chilli Pepper Sauce

**222**

- Replace the orange peppers with red peppers and add 2 finely chopped red chillies (chilies) to the frying pan.

### 223
**SERVES 4**

# Gruyère and Mushroom Cannelloni

PREPARATION TIME 10 MINUTES

COOKING TIME 35 MINUTES

#### INGREDIENTS

50 g / 1 ¾ oz / ¼ cup butter
2 shallots, chopped
2 cloves garlic, crushed
200 g / 7 oz / 2 cups button
mushrooms, chopped
12 sheets ready-made fresh pasta
2 tbsp plain (all purpose) flour
600 ml / 1 pint / 2 ½ cups milk
200 g / 7 oz / 2 cups Gruyère, grated

- Preheat the oven to 200°C (180°C fan) / 390F / gas 6.
- Melt half the butter in a frying pan and fry the shallots and garlic for 5 minutes. Add the mushrooms with a pinch of salt and cook for another 5 minutes.
- Meanwhile, melt the rest of the butter in a small saucepan. Stir in the flour then gradually incorporate the milk, stirring continuously.
- When it starts to bubble, stir in half the cheese and a grind of black pepper then take the pan off the heat.
- Add half the cheese sauce to the mushrooms and stir.
- Split the mushroom filling between the pasta sheets, then roll the up and pack them into a baking dish in a double layer.
- Pour over the rest of the sauce and sprinkle with the other half of the cheese.
- Bake the cannelloni for 20 minutes.

### Gorgonzola and Lardon Cannelloni
 224

- Replace the Gruyere with cubed Gorgonzola and fry 150 g / 5 oz / ¾ cup lardons, not mushrooms.

### 225
**SERVES 2**

# Ricotta and Olive Pizza

PREPARATION TIME 10 MINUTES

COOKING TIME 10 MINUTES

#### INGREDIENTS

1 large pizza base
3 tbsp tomato passata
100 g / 3 ½ oz / 1 cup ricotta
50 g / 1 ¾ oz / ⅔ cup mixed olives, pitted and sliced
2 tbsp caperberries
6 cherry tomatoes, halved
a handful rocket (arugula) leaves
salt and pepper

- Preheat the oven to 220°C (200°C fan) / 430F / gas 7 and put a baking tray in to heat.
- Spread the pizza base thinly with passata and crumble over the ricotta.
- Scatter over the olives and caperberries then arrange the tomato halves, cut side up.
- Give the top a good grind of black pepper then bake for 10 minutes or until the toppings are bubbling.
- Scatter over the rocket leaves and serve immediately.

### Ricotta, Olive and Anchovy Pizza  226
- Omit the tomatoes and add 4 chopped anchovy fillets instead.

# Pepperoni and Green Pepper Pizza

227

SERVES 2

## Pepperoni and Artichoke Pizza

228

- Replace the peppers with half a jar of preserved artichokes in oil.

## Green Pepper and Sweetcorn Pizza

229

- Omit the pepperoni and use 200 g / 7 oz / 1 ⅓ cup of canned sweetcorn instead.

PREPARATION TIME 8 MINUTES

COOKING TIME 10 MINUTES

### INGREDIENTS

1 large pizza base
3 tbsp passata sauce
100 g / 3 ½ oz / 1 cup mozzarella, sliced
100 g / 3 ½ oz / ⅔ cup pepperoni, sliced
½ green pepper, deseeded and sliced
a few sprigs mint

- Preheat the oven to 220°C (200°C fan) / 430F / gas 7 and put a baking tray in to heat.
- Spread the pizza base thinly with passata and arrange the mozzarella slices on top.
- Scatter over the pepperoni and green pepper and sprinkle with black pepper.
- Bake the pizza for 10 minutes or until the toppings are bubbling.
- Garnish with mint and serve immediately.

**230**

**SERVES 2**

# Tagliatelle with Broccoli and Parmesan

## Tagliatelle with Broccoli, Chilli and Anchovy

**231**

- Add a finely chopped red chilli (chili) and 4 chopped anchovy fillets in oil when you fry the garlic.

## Tagliatelle with Broccoli and Stilton

**232**

- Replace the Parmesan with 100 g / 3 ½ oz / ½ cup of cubed Stilton.

PREPARATION TIME 2 MINUTES

COOKING TIME 12 MINUTES

### INGREDIENTS

200 g / 7 oz / 2 cups tagliatelle
200 g / 7 oz / 1 ¼ cup broccoli, broken into small florets
4 tbsp olive oil
3 cloves garlic, crushed
2 tbsp basil, roughly chopped
75 g / 2 ½ oz / ¾ cup Parmesan, finely grated

- Cook the tagliatelle in boiling salted water according to the packet instructions or until al dente.
- Meanwhile, blanch the broccoli in boiling salted water for 3–4 minutes or until just tender. Drain well.
- Heat the oil in a sauté pan and fry the garlic for 2 minutes. Add the drained broccoli and cook, stirring occasionally, for 3 minutes so it can take on the flavour from the oil. Season to taste with salt and pepper.
- Reserve a couple of ladles of pasta water and drain the rest.
- Stir the pasta into the broccoli pan with the basil and 3 tablespoons of the pasta water and shake to emulsify with the oil. If it looks a bit dry, add some more pasta water.
- Divide between 2 warm bowls and top with plenty of Parmesan.

**233**

**SERVES 2**

# Linguini with Fresh Tomato Sauce

- Cook the linguini in boiling salted water according to the packet instructions or until al dente.
- While the pasta is cooking, score a cross in the top of each tomato and add them to the pasta water. When the skin of the tomatoes starts to curl up, remove them with a slotted spoon and dunk in a bowl of cold water.
- Peel off and discard the skins then chop the tomato flesh into small cubes.
- Mix the tomato in a bowl with the basil and olive oil and season well with salt and freshly ground black pepper.
- Drain the pasta and return it to the saucepan, then stir in the tomato dressing. Put the pan back over the heat for 1 minute to warm through.
- Divide the pasta between 2 bowls and sprinkle with Pecorino.

PREPARATION TIME 2 MINUTES

COOKING TIME 12 MINUTES

...........................................................

**INGREDIENTS**

200 g / 7 oz / 2 cups linguini
2 medium tomatoes
2 tbsp fresh basil leaves, shredded
6 tbsp extra virgin olive oil
50 g / 1 ¾ oz / ½ cup Pecorino, grated

## Linguini, Tomatoes and Olives

**234**

- Add 75 g / 3 oz / ½ cup of chopped, pitted kalamata olives and a finely chopped raw shallot to the tomatoes before dressing the pasta.

**235**

**SERVES 4**

# Stilton and Prosciutto Crustless Quiche

- Preheat the oven to 180°C (160°C fan) / 355F / gas 4.
- Lightly beat the eggs and mix them with the prosciutto, cheese and basil then season well with black pepper.
- Pour the mixture into a small baking dish and bake in the oven for 20–25 minutes or until just set in the centre.
- Serve warm or at room temperature.

PREPARATION TIME 2 MINUTES

COOKING TIME 15–20 MINUTES

...........................................................

**INGREDIENTS**

6 eggs
100 g / 3 ½ oz / ⅔ cup prosciutto
slices, chopped
100 g / 3 ½ oz / 1 cup Stilton, cubed
3 tbsp basil, finely shredded

## Mozzarella and Prosciutto Crustless Quiche

**236**

- Replace the Stilton with 150 g / 5 oz / 1 cup cubed Mozzarella and serve warm.

237

SERVES 4

# Rigatoni, Chicken and Apple Salad

PREPARATION TIME 5 MINUTES

COOKING TIME 12 MINUTES

### INGREDIENTS

200 g / 7 oz / 2 cups rigatoni pasta
3 tbsp mayonnaise
3 tbsp double (heavy) cream
1 tbsp lemon juice
2 tbsp French tarragon, leaves only
200 g / 7 oz / 2 cups / 1 ¾ cup pre-
cooked chicken breast, sliced
1 apple, cored and thinly sliced
1 head chicory, separated into leaves

- Cook the rigatoni in boiling salted water according to the packet instructions or until al dente.
- Drain well then plunge into iced water to cool for 5 minutes. Drain well.
- Meanwhile, mix the mayonnaise, cream and lemon juice together and stir in the tarragon. Season to taste with salt and pepper.
- Toss the rigatoni, chicken, apple and chicory with the dressing and divide between 4 serving bowls.

238

SERVES 4

# Penne with Smoked Salmon

PREPARATION TIME 2 MINUTES

COOKING TIME 25 MINUTES

### INGREDIENTS

400 g / 14 oz / 4 cups penne
2 tbsp butter
200 g / 7 oz / 2 ¼ cups chestnut
mushrooms, sliced
300 ml / 10 ½ oz / 1 ½ cup double
(heavy) cream
150 g / 5 ½ oz / 1 cup smoked
salmon, chopped
2 tbsp oregano or marjoram leaves
150 g / 5 ½ oz / 1 ½ cup Morbier
cheese, cubed

- Preheat the oven to 220°C (200°C fan) / 430F / gas 7.
- Cook the penne in boiling salted water according to the packet instructions or until al dente. Drain well.
- Meanwhile, melt the butter in a frying pan and cook the mushrooms with a pinch of salt for 10 minutes or until any liquid that comes out of them has evaporated and they start to brown.
- Add the double cream and bring to the boil then stir in the drained pasta, smoked salmon, herbs and Morbier.
- Spoon it into a baking dish and level the top then bake for 10 minutes or until the top is bubbling.

# Chicken Noodle Curry

SERVES 2

239

- Coat the chicken pieces with the curry paste and leave to marinate for 10 minutes.
- Meanwhile, cover the noodles in boiling water and leave to soften for 5 minutes. Drain well.
- Heat the oil in a wok and stir-fry the marinated chicken for 5 minutes or until cooked through.
- Add the coconut milk and bring to a simmer, then add the noodles and cook for 2 minutes or until tender.
- Garnish with coriander and serve.

PREPARATION TIME 10 MINUTES

COOKING TIME 10 MINUTES

## INGREDIENTS

2 skinless chicken breasts, sliced
2 tbsp Thai yellow curry paste
150 g / 5 ½ oz / 2 cups fine rice noodles
2 tbsp vegetable oil
200 ml / 7 fl. oz / ¾ cup coconut milk
2 tbsp coriander (cilantro) leaves, chopped

# Mushroom and Ham Cannelloni

240

SERVES 4

PREPARATION TIME 10 MINUTES

COOKING TIME 35 MINUTES

## INGREDIENTS

50 g / 1 ¾ oz / ¼ cup butter
2 shallots, chopped
2 cloves garlic, crushed
200 g / 7 oz / 2 ¼ cups button mushrooms, chopped
12 sheets ready-made fresh pasta
2 tbsp plain (all purpose) flour
600 ml / 1 pint / 2 ½ cup milk
200 g / 7 oz / 2 cups Emmental, grated
150 g / 5 ½ oz / 1 cup cooked ham, in small cubes
1 tbsp basil leaves, chopped

- Preheat the oven to 200°C (180°C fan) / 390F / gas 6.
- Melt half the butter in a frying pan and fry the shallots and garlic for 5 minutes. Add the mushrooms with a pinch of salt and cook for another 5 minutes.
- Meanwhile, melt the rest of the butter in a small saucepan. Stir in the flour then gradually incorporate the milk, stirring continuously to avoid any lumps forming.
- When the mixture starts to bubble, stir in half the cheese, the ham, basil and a grind of black pepper then take the pan off the heat.
- Add half of the sauce to the mushroom mixture and stir.
- Split the mushroom filling between the pasta sheets, then roll them up and pack them into 4 individual baking dishes.
- Pour over the rest of the sauce and sprinkle with the other half of the cheese.
- Bake the cannelloni for 20 minutes or until golden brown.

# Rigatoni with King Prawns

241

SERVES 4

PREPARATION TIME 2 MINUTES

COOKING TIME 12 MINUTES

## INGREDIENTS

400 g / 14 oz / 4 cups rigatoni
4 tbsp olive oil
2 shallots, finely chopped
2 cloves of garlic, crushed
200 g / 7 oz / 1 cup canned tomatoes, chopped
1 leek, trimmed, halved and thinly sliced
3 tbsp crème fraiche
300 g / 10 ½ oz / 1 ½ cup raw king prawns, peeled
flat leaf parsley to garnish

- Cook the rigatoni in boiling salted water according to the packet instructions or until al dente.
- While the pasta is cooking, heat half the oil in a frying pan and fry the shallots and garlic for 2 minutes. Add the canned tomatoes and bring to a simmer.
- Meanwhile, fry the leeks with a pinch of salt in the other half of the oil for 6 minutes or until very soft.
- Stir the crème fraiche into the tomato sauce and season to taste with salt and pepper.
- When the pasta is almost ready, add the prawns to the leeks and stir fry for 2 minutes or until they just turn opaque.
- Drain the pasta and divide it between 4 warm bowls.
- Spoon the tomato sauce over the pasta then top with the prawns and a few sprigs of parsley.

SERVES 2

# Maccheroncini and Chicken Salad

242

PREPARATION TIME 5 MINUTES

COOKING TIME 12 MINUTES

## INGREDIENTS

200 g / 7 oz / 2 cups maccheroncini
pasta
salt and pepper
1 tbsp lemon juice
3 tbsp extra virgin olive oil
100 g / 3 ½ oz / ¾ cup cooked
chicken breast, cubed
50 g / 1 ¾ oz / ⅓ cup cucumber,
halved and sliced
½ red pepper, deseeded and thinly
sliced
½ green pepper, deseeded and thinly
sliced
50 g / 1 ¾ oz / ⅓ cup black olives,
pitted and sliced
2 tbsp flat leaf parsley, chopped

- Cook the maccheroncini in boiling salted water according to the packet instructions or until al dente.
- Plunge it into cold water to stop the cooking then drain well.
- Whisk the lemon juice into the oil with a pinch of salt and toss it with the pasta.
- Stir in the chicken, cucumber, peppers, olives and parsley and serve at room temperature.

### Maccheroncini and Tuna Salad     243

- Replace the chicken with a jar of good quality white tuna in oil.

244

SERVES 4

# Farfalle with Spiced Winter Vegetables

PREPARATION TIME 5 MINUTES

COOKING TIME 20 MINUTES

## INGREDIENTS

2 carrots, cut into chunks
½ cauliflower, broken into florets
½ head broccoli, broken into florets
400 g / 14 oz / 4 cups farfalle pasta
4 tbsp olive oil
4 cloves garlic, crushed
½ tsp ground cumin
½ tsp ground coriander (cilantro)
½ tsp chilli (chili) flakes

- Bring a very large saucepan of water to the boil with half a tablespoon of salt.
- Add the carrots and cook for 2 minutes then add the cauliflower and broccoli and cook for a further 4 minutes.
- Remove the vegetables from the pan with a slotted spoon and leave to drain in a colander.
- Add the farfalle to the saucepan and cook according to the packet instructions or until al dente.
- While the pasta is cooking, heat the olive oil in a large sauté pan and cook the garlic and spices for 2 minutes, stirring regularly.
- Add the drained vegetables and toss to coat in the spiced oil. Add half a ladle of the pasta cooking water and simmer over a low heat.
- Drain the pasta and stir it into the sauté pan then divide it between 4 warm bowls.

### Farfalle and Spiced Vegetable Soup    245

- Add the pasta to the pan with enough of the cooking water to make a broth and sprinkle with Parmesan at the table.

246

SERVES 4

# Tuna Burgers

- Put the tuna in a food processor with the parsley, lemon zest and a pinch of salt and pepper and pulse until evenly mixed.
- Shape the mixture into 4 patties and chill in the fridge for 25 minutes or until firm.
- Preheat a griddle pan until smoking hot.
- Brush the burgers with oil and griddle for 8 minutes, turning them every 2 minutes.
- Serve the burgers with a lemon wedge on the side.

PREPARATION TIME 35 MINUTES

COOKING TIME 8 MINUTES

......................................................

### INGREDIENTS

450 g / 1 lb / 2 cups fresh tuna,
chopped
2 tbsp flat leaf parsley, chopped
1 lemon, zest finely grated
2 tbsp olive oil
lemon wedges to serve

## Moroccan Tuna Burgers

 247

- Replace the parsley with coriander leaves and add 1 tsp each of ras-al-hanout and harissa to the tuna before processing.

248

SERVES 2

# Turkey Baked with Bacon and Lemon

- Preheat the oven to 200°C (180°C fan) / 390F / gas 6.
- Line a baking dish with greaseproof paper and put the turkey breast on top.
- Arrange the lemon slices over the turkey and lay the bacon rashers on top.
- Drizzle over the olive oil and season well with salt and freshly ground black pepper.
- Fold the edges of the greaseproof paper over the top and bake for 30 minutes, peeling the paper back for the final 10 minutes.

PREPARATION TIME 5 MINUTES

COOKING TIME 30 MINUTES

......................................................

### INGREDIENTS

1 turkey breast
1 lemon, sliced
4 rashers smoked streaky bacon
3 tbsp olive oil
salt and pepper

## Turkey Breast
## with Lemon and Herbs

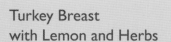 249

- Omit the bacon and lay a few sprigs of fresh rosemary, thyme and sage on top of the lemon slices instead.

**250**

**SERVES 2**

# Spaghetti with Roasted Vegetables

## Spaghetti with Roasted Squash

**251**

- Replace the vegetables with a cubed butternut squash and substitute the goats' cheese with Gorgonzola.

## Spaghetti with Watercress and Goats' Cheese

**252**

- Omit the roasted vegetable stage and use watercress instead of the rocket.

PREPARATION TIME 8 MINUTES

COOKING TIME 25 MINUTES

### INGREDIENTS

1 courgette (zucchini), halved and sliced
½ aubergine (eggplant), halved and sliced
1 red pepper, deseeded and cut into strips
1 yellow pepper, deseeded and cut into strips
4 tbsp olive oil
200 g / 7 oz / 2 cups spaghetti
100 g / 3 ½ oz / ⅔ cup fresh goats' cheese
30 g / 1 oz / 1 cup rocket (arugula) leaves

- Preheat the oven to 220°C (200°C fan) / 430F / gas 7.
- Rub the vegetables with oil and season well with salt and pepper then spread them out in a large roasting tin. Roast for 25 minutes, turning half way through.
- Once you've turned the vegetables, cook the spaghetti in boiling salted water according to the packet instructions or until al dente.
- Drain the pasta then stir it into the roasting tin to absorb some of the flavours.
- Divide the pasta and vegetables between 2 warm plates and crumble over the goats' cheese.
- Top with the rocket leaves and serve immediately.

**253**

**SERVES 4**

# Pepper, Bacon and Mussel Kebabs

- Put 12 wooden skewers in a bowl of cold water and leave to soak for 20 minutes.
- Mix the oil with the oregano and drizzle it over the peppers, bacon and mussels. Leave to marinate for 20 minutes.
- Preheat the grill to its highest setting.
- Thread alternate pieces of red pepper, bacon and mussels onto the skewers.
- Grill the kebabs for 4 minutes on each side or until cooked and golden.
- Meanwhile, fry the mushrooms and oregano in the oil with a pinch of salt for 8 minutes or until any liquid that comes out has evaporated and they start to take on some colour.
- Serve the kebabs on a bed of fried mushrooms.

PREPARATION TIME 30 MINUTES

COOKING TIME 8 MINUTES

**INGREDIENTS**

4 tbsp olive oil
1 tsp dried oregano
3 red peppers, deseeded and cut into large chunks
8 rashers streaky bacon, cut into large squares
450 g / 1 lb / 1 ½ cups cooked shelled mussels

FOR THE MUSHROOMS
300 g / 10 ½ oz / 4 cups mushrooms, sliced
1 tsp dried oregano
3 tbsp olive oil

### Bacon, Mussel and Mushroom Kebabs

**254**

- Instead of serving the kebabs on a bed of mushrooms, thread the whole mushrooms onto the skewers and omit the peppers.

**255**

**SERVES 4**

# Chicken, Pepper and Lemon Kebabs

- Put 12 wooden skewers in a bowl of water and leave to soak for 20 minutes.
- Meanwhile, stir the paprika into the oil and toss it with the chicken, lemon and vegetables.
- Leave to marinate for 20 minutes.
- Preheat the grill to its highest setting.
- Thread alternate chunks of chicken, lemon and vegetables onto the skewers and spread them out on a large grill tray.
- Grill the kebabs for 4 minutes on each side or until they are golden brown and cooked through.
- Garnish with thyme before serving.

PREPARATION TIME 25 MINUTES

COOKING TIME 8 MINUTES

**INGREDIENTS**

½ tsp smoked paprika
4 tbsp olive oil
6 skinless chicken breasts, cubed
1 lemon, sliced
1 red pepper, deseeded and cubed
1 green pepper, deseeded and cubed
1 onion, cut into chunks
12 cherry tomatoes
a few thyme sprigs to garnish

### Lamb, Pepper and Lemon Kebabs

**256**

- Replace the chicken with 450 g / 1 lb / 2 cups of cubed lamb neck fillet.

**257**

**SERVES 4**

# Lamb Chops with Potatoes and Gravy

**PREPARATION TIME 2 MINUTES**

**COOKING TIME 20 MINUTES**

### INGREDIENTS

800 g / 1 lb 12 oz / 4 ½ cups maris piper potatoes, peeled and cut into chunks
8 lamb chops
2 tbsp olive oil
salt and pepper
a few sprigs oregano

### FOR THE GRAVY
1 large onion, finely chopped
2 tbsp butter
2 tbsp Madeira
250 ml / 9 fl. oz / 1 cup lamb stock

- Preheat the grill to its highest setting.
- Boil the potatoes in salted water for 12 minutes then drain well and leave to steam dry for 2 minutes.
- Meanwhile, fry the onion in the butter for 10 minutes or until starting to caramelise.
- Add the Madeira and a pinch of salt and bubble away almost to nothing.
- Add the lamb stock and simmer gently until reduced and slightly thickened.
- Brush the chops with oil and season with salt and pepper then grill for 3 minutes on each side.
- Arrange the potatoes on 4 warm plates and add 2 lamb chops to each.
- Strain the gravy through a sieve to get rid of the onions and spoon it around the plate.
- Garnish the plates with oregano sprigs.

**258**

**SERVES 2**

# Prawn, Coconut and Lime Leaf Skewers

**PREPARATION TIME 5 MINUTES**

**COOKING TIME 4 MINUTES**

### INGREDIENTS

20 raw king prawns, peeled
8 frozen lime leaves, defrosted
1 tbsp vegetable oil
30 g / 1 oz / ¼ cup creamed coconut block, grated

- Preheat a griddle pan until smoking hot.
- Thread the prawns and lime leaves onto 8 metal skewers.
- Stir the oil into the creamed coconut and brush it over the prawns then griddle the skewers for 2 minutes on each side or until the prawns turn opaque.

## 259

**SERVES 4**

# Lamb Kebabs with Cucumber Salad

- Soak 4 wooden skewers in cold water for 20 minutes.
- Stir the oregano into 3 tbsp of the oil and toss it with the lamb and peppers. Leave to marinate for 15 minutes.
- Meanwhile, toss the cucumber with the vinegar, remaining oil and sesame seeds. Season well with salt and pepper and leave to drain in a sieve for 15 minutes.
- Preheat the grill to its highest setting.
- Thread alternate chunks of lamb and peppers onto the skewers and spread them out on a large grill tray.
- Grill the kebabs for 4 minutes on each side or until they are golden brown and cooked through.
- Split open the pitta breads and fill them with cucumber salad.
- Top each one with a kebab and serve.

PREPARATION TIME 25 MINUTES

COOKING TIME 8 MINUTES

### INGREDIENTS

1 tsp dried oregano
4 tbsp olive oil
450 g / 1 lb / 2 cups lamb leg, cubed
½ green pepper, deseeded and cubed
½ red pepper, deseeded and cubed
½ yellow pepper, deseeded and cubed
4 pitta breads
½ cucumber, julienned
2 tbsp white wine vinegar
1 tsp sesame seeds

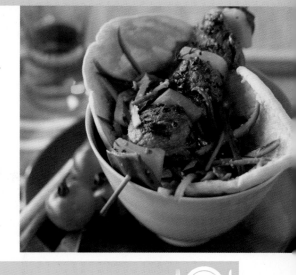

# Duck with Onions and Honey

## 260

**SERVES 2**

PREPARATION TIME 5 MINUTES

COOKING TIME 18 MINUTES

### INGREDIENTS

2 small duck breasts, skin slashed
6 large spring onions (scallions), trimmed
a few sprigs rosemary

1 tbsp white wine vinegar
3 tbsp white wine
1 tbsp runny honey
½ tsp pink peppercorns, crushed

- Preheat the oven to 200°C (180°C fan) / 390F / gas 6.
- Put the duck breast, skin side down, in a cold ovenproof frying pan, then put the pan on the hob and turn the heat up high.
- Cook the duck without disturbing for 8 minutes. When the skin side is golden brown, turn the duck over, add the onions and rosemary to the pan. Season well then transfer to the oven for 6 minutes.
- Leave the duck, onions and all but 1 sprig of rosemary to rest on a warm plate, covered with a double layer of foil.
- Pour off all but 1 tbsp of the duck fat into a ramekin, then put the pan back on the heat and add the vinegar and wine. Reduce the liquid by half then stir in the honey.
- Finely chop the rosemary and add it to the sauce.
- Put the duck breasts on 2 warm plates and divide the onions and crisp rosemary sprigs between them.
- Spoon over the sauce and sprinkle with pink peppercorns.

# Monkfish and Pepper Kebabs

## 261

**SERVES 4**

PREPARATION TIME 20 MINUTES

COOKING TIME 8 MINUTES

### INGREDIENTS

450 g / 1 lb / 2 ¼ cups monkfish, boned and cubed
½ green pepper, deseeded and cubed

½ red pepper, deseeded and cubed
½ yellow pepper, deseeded and cubed
2 tbsp flat leaf parsley, chopped

- Soak 4 wooden skewers in cold water for 20 minutes.
- Preheat the grill to its highest setting.
- Thread alternate chunks of monkfish and peppers onto the skewers and spread them out on a large grill tray.
- Grill the kebabs for 4 minutes on each side or until they are golden brown and cooked through.
- Sprinkle with parsley and serve.

**262**

**SERVES 2**

# Steak with Garlic Sauce and Parsnip Chips

PREPARATION TIME 10 MINUTES

COOKING TIME 18 MINUTES

### INGREDIENTS

2 skirt or flash-fry steaks
1 tbsp olive oil
salt and pepper

**FOR THE SAUCE**

1 tbsp butter
2 cloves garlic, finely chopped
½ tsp cracked black peppercorns
1 tbsp brandy
200 ml / 7 fl. oz / ¾ cup double (heavy) cream

**FOR THE PARSNIP CHIPS**

3 parsnips, cut into long chips
2–3 litres / 3 ½–5 pints / 8–12 cups sunflower oil

- Heat the oil in a deep fat fryer, according to the manufacturer's instructions, to a temperature of 130°C. Fry the parsnips for 10 minutes without browning.
- Brush the steaks with oil and season. Fry in a smoking hot frying pan for 2 minutes on each side. Transfer the steaks to a warm plate, wrapped in a double layer of foil.
- Pull up the fryer basket and increase the temperature to 190°C. Cook the chips for 2–3 minutes at the hotter temperature or until crisp and golden brown.
- Tip the chips into a bowl with kitchen paper to remove oil. Return the pan to the heat and add the butter.
- Fry the garlic and peppercorns for 1 minute then add the brandy and cream and bubble for 1 minute.
- Transfer the steaks to 2 warm plates and stir any juices into the sauce.
- Arrange the parsnips next to the steaks and spoon the sauce over the top.

## Steak with Vegetable Chips

 263

- Instead of parsnips, you could make a mixture of vegetable chips using sweet potatoes, carrots and butternut squash.

**264**

**SERVES 2**

# Cod with Prosciutto and Cabbage

PREPARATION TIME 5 MINUTES

COOKING TIME 10 MINUTES

### INGREDIENTS

2 tbsp olive oil
2 thick portions cod fillet
2 slices prosciutto
2 tbsp flat leaf parsley, chopped
½ small hispi cabbage, sliced
1 tbsp butter
salt and pepper

- Preheat the oven to 200°C (180°C fan) / 390F / gas 6 and bring a large pan of salted water to the boil.
- Heat the oil in an oven proof frying pan. Season the cod with salt and pepper and fry, skin side down, for 4 minutes.
- Turn the pieces of cod over and sprinkle with parsley and lay the prosciutto slices next to them in the pan.
- Transfer the pan to the oven and cook for 5 minutes or until the prosciutto is crisp and the cod is just cooked in the centre.
- Boil the cabbage for 3 minutes or until tender then drain well. Stir in the butter and season with salt and pepper.
- Divide the cabbage between 2 warm plates and top with the cod and crispy prosciutto.

## Chicken with Prosciutto and Cabbage

265

- Replace the cod with 2 skin-on chicken breasts.

# Boudin Blanc with Caramelised Apples

**266**

**SERVES 4**

- Heat the oil in a large frying pan and fry the sausages over a low heat for 15 minutes, turning occasionally.
- Halfway through the cooking time, add the apples to the pan, turning them once.
- Remove the sausages from the pan and keep warm.
- Stir the vinegar into the honey then add it to the pan with the apples and bubble to a sticky glaze.
- Transfer the apples to a serving plate and top with the boudin blanc.

PREPARATION TIME 2 MINUTES

COOKING TIME 20 MINUTES

### INGREDIENTS

2 tbsp olive oil
4 boudin blanc sausages
2 eating apples, cored and sliced
1 tbsp cider vinegar
1 tbsp runny honey

### Fennel Sausages with Caramelised Pears

**267**

- Substitute Italian-style fennel sausages for the boudin blanc and replace the apples with pears.

# Sea Bass Fillet with Potato and Thyme

**268**

**SERVES 2**

- Boil the potatoes in salted water for 8 minutes then drain well and leave to steam dry for 2 minutes.
- Heat 4 tbsp of the oil in a large sauté pan.
- Season the potatoes then fry for 10 minutes, shaking the pan and stirring occasionally.
- Meanwhile, heat the rest of the oil in a frying pan. Season the sea bass and lower the fillets into the pan, skin side down.
- Cook for 4 minutes or until the skin is golden brown and crisp, then turn them over and sprinkle in the thyme.
- Cook for 2 minutes or until the centre is just cooked.
- Transfer the bass to 2 warm plates and spoon over the potatoes.
- Wrap the lime halves in muslin to catch any pips and put them on the side of the plates.

PREPARATION TIME 5 MINUTES

COOKING TIME 25 MINUTES

### INGREDIENTS

6 tbsp olive oil
400 g / 14 oz / 2 ¼ cups charlotte potatoes, peeled and cubed
salt and pepper
1 large sea bass, filleted and pin boned
2 tbsp fresh thyme leaves
1 lime, halved

### Barbecued Bream with Sautéed Potatoes

**269**

- Serve the potatoes with sea bream that have been barbecued whole.

## 270

**SERVES 4**

# Pork Belly with Fennel and Chestnuts

PREPARATION TIME 5 MINUTES

COOKING TIME 40 MINUTES

### INGREDIENTS

2 fennel bulbs, thickly sliced
200 g / 7 oz / 1 ⅔ cups whole
chestnuts, cooked and peeled
1 tbsp olive oil
800 g / 1 lb 12 oz / 5 cups boneless
pork belly, skin scored
30 g / 1 oz / ¼ cup fresh white
breadcrumbs

- Preheat the oven to 230°C (210°C fan) / 450F / gas 8.
- Rub the fennel and chestnuts with oil and arrange them in a roasting tin.
- Put the pork on top, skin side up, and roast for 35 minutes.
- Take the pork out and leave it to rest in a warm place for 5 minutes.
- Meanwhile, sprinkle the fennel and chestnuts with breadcrumbs and return them to the oven for 5 minutes.
- Cut the pork into 4 thick slices and serve with the fennel and chestnuts.

### Roast Pork with Red Onions

 271

- Replace the fennel with 2 large sliced red onions and a few sprigs of rosemary. Omit the chestnuts.

## 272

**SERVES 4**

# Crusted Lamb with Fondant Potatoes

PREPARATION TIME 10 MINUTES

COOKING TIME 20 MINUTES

### INGREDIENTS

1 tbsp hazelnuts (cob nuts), chopped
1 tsp coriander (cilantro) seeds
2 tbsp flat leaf parsley
3 tbsp Parmesan, grated
1–2 tbsp olive oil
8 lamb chops
salt and pepper
150 g / 5 ½ oz / 1 cup frozen peas

FOR THE POTATOES

1 large baking potato, peeled
2 tbsp butter
250 ml / 9 fl. oz / 1 cup lamb stock

- Mix the hazelnuts, coriander seeds, parsley and parmesan and stir in enough oil to make a stiff paste.
- Spread the paste onto the lamb and preheat the grill to its highest setting.
- Cut the ends off the potato then cut it into 4 thick slices. Melt the butter in a small frying pan and fry the potatoes for 3 minutes on one side or until browned.
- Cook for 3 minutes on the other side, then pour in the lamb stock. Cover the pan and cook for 5 minutes then turn the potatoes and cook uncovered for 5 minutes.
- Meanwhile, spread the lamb out on a grill tray and season. Grill the chops for 3 minutes on each side.
- Boil the peas for 4 minutes then drain. Arrange the potatoes and chops on 4 plates.
- Divide the peas between the plates and drizzle over any stock left in the potato pan.

### Crusted Pork Chops

 273

- Use pork chops instead of lamb chops and replace the parsley in the crust with sage leaves.

274

**SERVES 2**

# Griddled Pork and Aubergine

## Griddled Gammon and Aubergines

 275

- Soak 2 gammon steaks in pineapple juice for 20 minutes then blot them dry and use in place of the pork.

## Griddled Pork and Courgettes

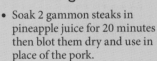 276

- Use 4 sliced courgettes instead of the aubergine, adding them to the griddle pan half way through the cooking time.

PREPARATION TIME 15 MINUTES

COOKING TIME 8 MINUTES

### INGREDIENTS

1 aubergine (eggplant), sliced lengthways
salt
2 pork fillet steaks
2 tomatoes, halved
4 tbsp olive oil
a few sprigs thyme
½ tsp pink peppercorns, crushed

- Sprinkle the aubergine slices with salt and leave them for 5 minutes to draw the moisture out.
- Blot them well with kitchen paper.
- Preheat a large griddle pan until smoking hot.
- Brush the aubergine, pork and tomatoes with oil and sprinkle over the thyme and pink peppercorns.
- Season everything with sea salt at the last minute then griddle for 4 minutes on each side or until nicely marked and the pork is cooked through.

## 277
**SERVES 2**

# Chicken Escalope with Sautéed Vegetables

PREPARATION TIME 5 MINUTES

COOKING TIME 18 MINUTES

### INGREDIENTS

2 tbsp fresh thyme leaves
2 tbsp olive oil
black pepper
2 chicken escalopes

### FOR THE VEGETABLES

2 tbsp olive oil
100 g / 3 ½ oz / 1 cup baby button
onions, peeled
100 g / 3 ½ oz / ½ cup lardons
100 g / 3 ½ oz / 1 cup baby button
mushrooms
100 g / 3 ½ oz / 1 cup sugar snap peas
½ lemon, juiced

- Mix the thyme with the oil and some freshly ground black pepper and brush it over the chicken. Leave to marinate for 10 minutes.
- Heat the oil in a large sauté pan and fry the onions and lardons for 5 minutes. Add the mushrooms and cook for another 5 minutes, then add the sugar snap peas and cook for a final 3 minutes. Stir in the lemon juice.
- Meanwhile, preheat a griddle pan until smoking hot.
- Griddle the chicken for 3 minutes on each side or until nicely marked and cooked through.
- Divide the vegetables between 2 warm plates and serve the chicken on top.

### Turkey Escalope with Sautéed Vegetables

278

- Replace the chicken with turkey and use finely shredded sage leaves instead of thyme.

## 279
**SERVES 4**

# Steak Skewers with Corn on the Cob

PREPARATION TIME 20 MINUTES

COOKING TIME 15 MINUTES

### INGREDIENTS

1 tsp orange zest, finely grated
1 tbsp flat leaf parsley, finely
chopped
2 tbsp olive oil
salt and pepper
4 minute steaks, halved lengthways
4 sweetcorn cobs, halved

- Soak 8 wooden skewers in cold water for 20 minutes.
- Stir the orange zest and parsley into the oil with plenty of freshly ground black pepper and brush it over the steak. Leave to marinate for 15 minutes.
- Meanwhile, boil the sweetcorn in salted water for 8 minutes. Drain well.
- Preheat a large griddle pan until smoking hot.
- Thread each piece of steak onto a skewer and arrange on the griddle with the corn.
- Cook for 3 minutes on each side or until nicely marked.

### Satay Beef Skewers

280

- Mix 2 tbsp of crunchy peanut butter with 1 tbsp of soy sauce and 1 tsp each of honey and Chinese 5 spice and massage into the beef instead of the orange and parsley.

**SERVES 4**

# Red Mullet with Salad

- Put the couscous and garlic in a bowl and pour over 100 ml / 3 ½ fl. oz / ½ cup of boiling water.
- Cover the bowl with clingfilm and let it stand for 5 minutes then fluff up the grains with a fork.
- Season the couscous with salt and pepper and stir in the pine nuts and mint.
- Preheat a grill to its highest setting.
- Stuff the stomach cavities of the mullet with the couscous mixture and arrange them on a large grill tray.
- Grill the fish for 4 minutes on each side or until cooked through.
- Meanwhile, whisk together the honey, lemon juice and oil with a pinch of salt and use it to dress the onion and tomatoes.
- Divide the salad between 4 plates and top each one with 2 mullet.

PREPARATION TIME 15 MINUTES

COOKING TIME 8 MINUTES

**INGREDIENTS**

100 g / 3 ½ oz / ⅔ cup couscous
½ clove garlic, crushed
salt and pepper
1 tbsp pine nuts
1 tbsp mint, chopped
8 red mullet, gutted

FOR THE SALAD
1 tsp runny honey
½ lemon, juiced
3 tbsp olive oil
1 red onion, sliced
2 tomatoes, cut into wedges

## Stuffed Sea Bream

282

- Use the couscous to stuff 1 small sea bream per person. You may need to increase the cooking time to 5 minutes per side.

**SERVES 4**

# Chicken and Rosemary Skewers

- Heat the oil in a sauté pan and fry the leeks, celery and courgettes for 10 minutes to soften. Add the garlic and cook for 2 more minutes, then stir in the wine and cook until almost evaporated.
- Meanwhile, preheat the grill to its highest setting.
- Strip most of the leaves off the rosemary sprigs and thread the chicken onto the woody stems like a skewer.
- Brush the chicken with oil and season with salt and pepper then grill for 4 minutes on each side or until cooked through.
- Divide the vegetables between 4 warm bowls and top each one with 2 chicken skewers. Garnish with chervil.

PREPARATION TIME 25 MINUTES

COOKING TIME 30 MINUTES

**INGREDIENTS**

8 woody sprigs of rosemary
2 skinless chicken breasts, cubed
2 tbsp olive oil
salt and pepper
a few sprigs of chervil to garnish

FOR THE VEGETABLES
4 tbsp olive oil
1 leek, cleaned and chopped
2 sticks celery, cubed
2 courgettes (zucchini), cubed
2 cloves of garlic, crushed
100 ml / 3 ½ fl. oz / ½ cup white wine

## Lamb and Rosemary Skewers

284

- Replace the chicken with chunks of lamb neck fillet, making the holes with a metal skewer first before threading it onto the rosemary.

**285**

**MAKES 6**

# Mediterranean Chicken Burgers

PREPARATION TIME 35 MINUTES

COOKING TIME 12 MINUTES

### INGREDIENTS

600 g / 1 lb 5 oz / 2 ⅔ cups chicken
thigh meat, chopped
1 clove of garlic, crushed
1 tbsp lemon zest, finely grated
25 g / 1 oz Parmesan, finely grated
a small bunch basil, chopped
2 tbsp olive oil
lemon wedges, to serve

- Put all of the ingredients except the oil into a food processor and pulse until finely chopped and evenly mixed.
- Shape the mixture into 6 thin patties and layer between sheets of greaseproof paper.
- Chill for 30 minutes to firm up.
- Heat the oil in a large frying pan and fry the burgers in 2 batches for 3 minutes on each side or until cooked through and golden brown. Serve with lemon wedges.

### Mediterranean Mackerel Burgers  286

- Replace the chicken with an equal weight of boneless, skinless mackerel fillet.

**287**

**SERVES 4**

# Rack of Lamb with Peas

PREPARATION TIME 5 MINUTES

COOKING TIME 20 MINUTES

### INGREDIENTS

2 x 6-bone racks of lamb
2 tbsp olive oil
salt and pepper
150 g / 5 ½ oz / 1 ½ cups sugar snap
peas
150 g / 5 ½ oz / 1 cup fresh peas,
podded
a few sprigs fresh coriander (cilantro)

### FOR THE GRAVY

1 large onion, finely chopped
2 tbsp butter
2 tbsp Madeira
250 ml / 9 fl. oz / 1 cup good quality
lamb stock

- Preheat the oven to 220°C (200°C fan) / 430F / gas 7 and heat a frying pan until smoking hot.
- Brush the lamb with oil and sear it all over in the frying pan, then season and roast in the oven for 10 minutes. Leave the lamb to rest for 5 minutes.
- Meanwhile, fry the onion in the butter for 10 minutes.
- Add the Madeira and a pinch of salt and bubble away almost to nothing. Add the lamb stock and simmer gently until reduced and slightly thickened.
- While the gravy is cooking, boil the sugar snaps and peas for 4 minutes or until al dente.
- Cut the lamb into individual chops and serve 3 per person on a bed of peas and sugar snaps.
- Strain the gravy through a sieve to get rid of the onions and spoon it around the plate.
- Garnish the lamb with coriander.

### Rack of Lamb with Onion Gravy 288

- Thinly slice the onions instead of chopping them and don't strain the gravy.

**289**
**SERVES 2**

# Salmon with Peppers and Tartare Sauce

### Mackerel with Peppers and Tartare Sauce

**290**

- Substitute the salmon with whole grilled mackerel.

### Poached Salmon with Tartare Sauce

**291**

- Poach the salmon instead of frying it and serve without the pepper garnish.

PREPARATION TIME 8 MINUTES

COOKING TIME 6 MINUTES

### INGREDIENTS

2 portions salmon fillet
2 tbsp olive oil
salt and pepper
1 jar roasted peppers in oil, drained
1 tbsp walnuts, chopped
1 tbsp fresh dill, chopped

### FOR THE TARTARE SAUCE
3 tbsp mayonnaise
2 gherkins, finely chopped
1 tsp baby capers
½ shallot, finely chopped
2 tsp lemon juice

- Preheat a frying pan until smoking hot.
- Brush the salmon fillets with the oil and season with salt and pepper.
- Fry the salmon for 3 minutes on each side.
- Meanwhile, mix the peppers with the walnuts and dill and season with salt and pepper.
- To make the tartare sauce, stir the ingredients together with a little freshly ground black pepper.
- Serve the salmon on a bed of red peppers with a spoonful of tartare sauce on the side.

**292**

**SERVES 4**

# Roasted Vegetable Crustless Quiche

PREPARATION TIME 2 MINUTES

COOKING TIME 40–45 MINUTES

.......................................................

### INGREDIENTS

1 courgette (zucchini), cut
into chunks
1 aubergine (eggplant) , cut
into chunks
1 red pepper, deseeded and cut into
chunks
1 yellow pepper, deseeded and cut
into chunks
2 tbsp olive oil
salt and pepper
6 eggs
1 tbsp basil, finely shredded

- Preheat the oven to 180°C (160°C fan) / 355F / gas 4.
- Rub the vegetables with oil and season with salt and
  pepper then roast for 20 minutes.
- Lightly beat the eggs and stir in the vegetables.
- Pour the mixture into a small baking dish and bake
  in the oven for 20–25 minutes or until just set in the
  centre.
- Sprinkle with basil and serve warm or at room
  temperature.

### Roasted Onion Crustless Quiche  293

- Replace the vegetables with
  2 red onions, cut into eighths.

**294**

**SERVES 4**

# Pea and Asparagus Crustless Quiche

PREPARATION TIME 5 MINUTES

COOKING TIME 20–25 MINUTES

.......................................................

### INGREDIENTS

6 eggs
100 g / 3 ½ oz / ⅔ cup frozen peas,
defrosted
salt and black pepper
1 jar white asparagus, drained

### FOR THE SALSA
1 shallot, finely chopped
1 mild green chilli (chili), chopped
3 tomatoes, diced
100 g / 3 ½ oz / ½ cup cooked brown
shrimp, peeled

- Preheat the oven to 180°C (160°C fan) / 355F / gas 4.
- Lightly beat the eggs and mix them with the peas then
  season well with salt and black pepper.
- Pour the mixture into a small baking dish and lay the
  asparagus across the top then bake in the oven for
  20–25 minutes or until just set in the centre.
- Meanwhile, mix together the salsa ingredients and
  season to taste with salt and black pepper.

### Shrimp and Tomato Bruschetta  295

- Use the salsa to top slices of
  toasted sourdough bread.

## 296

**SERVES 4**

# Crispy Sesame and Poppy Seed Sole

- Mix the poppy seeds and sesame seeds together in a bowl then put the cornflour and egg white in 2 separate bowls.
- Dip the sole fillets first in the cornflour, then in egg white, then in the seeds to coat.
- Heat the oil in a deep fat fryer, according to the manufacturer's instructions, to a temperature of 180°C.
- Lower the sole in the fryer basket and cook for 4–5 minutes or until crisp and golden brown.
- Line a large bowl with a thick layer of kitchen paper and when they are ready, tip them into the bowl to remove any excess oil.
- Sprinkle with a little sea salt to taste and serve immediately with the mixed leaves and petals.

PREPARATION TIME 10 MINUTES

COOKING TIME 4–5 MINUTES

**INGREDIENTS**

50 g / 2 ½ oz / 1 cup poppy seeds
50 g / 2 ½ oz / 1 cup sesame seeds
4 tbsp cornflour (cornstarch)
1 egg white, beaten
12 small sole fillets
2–3 litres / 3 ½–5 pints / 8–12 cups sunflower oil
sea salt
mixed salad leaves and flower petals to serve

### Beer-battered Sole

297

- Make a batter for the sole instead: stir enough fizzy beer into 50 g / 2 oz / ⅓ cup of plain (all purpose) flour to make it the consistency of double (heavy) cream.

## 298

**SERVES 4**

# Farfalle, Broad Bean and Pesto Salad

- Cook the farfalle in boiling salted water according to the packet instructions or until al dente, adding the broad beans to the pan for the last 6 minutes.
- Drain the pasta and broad beans and toss with the tomato, pesto and olive oil.
- Use a vegetable peeler to shave over some Parmesan and garnish with sprigs of basil.

PREPARATION TIME 8 MINUTES

COOKING TIME 12 MINUTES

**INGREDIENTS**

400 g / 14 oz / 4 cups farfalle pasta
200 g / 7 oz / 1 ¾ cup broad beans, podded weight
1 tomato, diced
4 tbsp pesto
3 tbsp olive oil
30 g / 1 oz Parmesan
a few sprigs basil

### Farfalle, Asparagus and Pesto Salad

299

- Replace the broad beans with asparagus spears, cut into short lengths.

**300**

**SERVES 2**

# Mushrooms with Bacon and Chestnuts

PREPARATION TIME 5 MINUTES

COOKING TIME 18 MINUTES

### INGREDIENTS

200 g / 7 oz / 2 cups mixed wild mushrooms (to include chanterelles, ceps and wood blewits)
1 tbsp olive oil
2 shallots, finely chopped
2 thick rashers streaky bacon, sliced
1 tbsp butter
salt and pepper
1 clove of garlic, crushed
100 g / 3 ½ oz / ¾ cup whole chestnuts, cooked and peeled
1 tbsp flat leaf parsley, chopped

- Pick over the mushrooms and brush away any soil with a pastry brush. Cut the bigger mushrooms into bite-sized pieces.
- Heat the olive oil in a large sauté pan and fry the shallots and bacon for 4 minutes.
- Add the mushrooms to the pan with the butter, season with salt and pepper and cook for 10 minutes, stirring occasionally.
- When all of the liquid that comes out of the mushrooms has evaporated and they start to colour, add the garlic, chestnuts and parsley and cook for another minute or two.

### Wild Mushrooms with Walnuts  301

- Replace the chestnuts with 75 g / 3 oz / ⅔ cup of walnut halves.

**302**

**SERVES 4**

# Stir-fried Beef with Vegetables

PREPARATION TIME 5 MINUTES

COOKING TIME 15 MINUTES

### INGREDIENTS

4 tbsp vegetable oil
1 aubergine (eggplant), peeled and cubed
2 cloves garlic, finely chopped
1 tbsp root ginger, finely chopped
200 g / 7 oz / 1 ¼ cups sirloin steak, thinly sliced
75 g / 2 ½ oz / ½ cup baby sweetcorn, chopped
1 carrot, julienned
1 courgette (zucchini), julienned
1 red pepper, deseeded and julienned
½ tsp cornflour (cornstarch)
2 tbsp rice wine or dry sherry
1 tsp caster (superfine) sugar
1 tbsp light soy sauce
75 g / 2 ½ oz / ¾ cup bean sprouts
a few sprigs coriander (cilantro)

- Heat half the oil in a large wok and stir-fry the aubergine for 4 minutes or until golden. Remove from the wok with a slotted spoon and reserve.
- Heat the rest of the oil and fry the garlic and ginger for 30 seconds.
- Add the steak and stir-fry for 2 minutes then add the baby corn and carrot and stir-fry for another 2 minutes.
- Add the courgette and pepper and return the aubergine to the pan. Stir-fry for 2 more minutes.
- Mix the cornflour with the rice wine, sugar and soy and add it to the wok with the bean sprouts.
- Stir-fry for 1 more minute then serve immediately, garnished with the coriander.

### Stir-fried Duck with Vegetables  303

- Replace the beef with 2 thinly sliced duck breasts.

304

SERVES 4

# Stir-fried Pork with Peppers and Cabbage

## Two Cabbage Stir-fry

 305

- Omit the pork and add ¼ a thinly shredded red cabbage to the wok when you add the Chinese cabbage.

## Stir-fried Pork with Mushrooms

306

- Replace the cabbage and peppers with 300 g / 11 oz / 3 cups of sliced button mushrooms.

PREPARATION TIME 5 MINUTES

COOKING TIME 8 MINUTES

......................................................

### INGREDIENTS

3 tbsp vegetable oil
2 cloves garlic, finely chopped
1 tbsp root ginger, finely chopped
200 g / 7 oz / 1 ¼ cups pork steak, thinly sliced
1 carrot, julienned
1 red pepper, deseeded and julienned
1 yellow pepper, deseeded and julienned
½ Chinese cabbage, chopped
2 tbsp oyster sauce
1 tbsp light soy sauce
75 g / 2 ½ oz / ¾ cup bean sprouts

- Heat the oil in a large wok and fry the garlic and ginger for 30 seconds.
- Add the pork and stir-fry for 2 minutes then add the carrots and peppers and stir-fry for another 2 minutes.
- Add the cabbage and stir-fry for 2 more minutes.
- Mix the oyster sauce with the soy and 2 tablespoons of water and add it to the wok with the bean sprouts.
- Stir-fry for 1 more minute then serve immediately.

**307**

**SERVES 4**

# Chicken with Pineapple and Tomatoes

PREPARATION TIME 5 MINUTES

COOKING TIME 6–8 MINUTES

......................................................

## INGREDIENTS

3 tbsp vegetable oil
2 cloves garlic, finely chopped
1 tbsp root ginger, finely chopped
225 g / 8 oz / 1 ½ cups chicken breast, sliced
½ fresh pineapple, peeled and cut into chunks
2 tbsp rice wine or dry sherry
1 tsp caster (superfine) sugar
1 tbsp light soy sauce
100 g / 3 ½ oz / ¾ cup cherry tomatoes, halved
4 spring onions (scallions), sliced diagonally

- Heat the oil in a large wok and fry the garlic and ginger for 30 seconds.
- Add the chicken and stir-fry for 2 minutes then add the pineapple and stir-fry for another 2 minutes.
- Mix the rice wine, sugar and soy together and add it to the wok with the tomatoes and spring onion.
- Stir-fry for 2 more minutes then serve immediately.

### Duck with Pineapple and Tomatoes

**308**

- Replace the chicken with duck breast.

---

**309**

**SERVES 4**

# Stir-fried Squid with Chilli and Spinach

PREPARATION TIME 5 MINUTES

COOKING TIME 5 MINUTES

......................................................

## INGREDIENTS

100 g / 3 ½ oz / 3 ¼ cups baby leaf spinach
2 tbsp vegetable oil
2 cloves garlic, finely chopped
2 red chillies (chilies), thinly sliced
300 g / 10 ½ oz / 2 cups raw squid rings
½ lemon, juiced
2 tsp light soy sauce

- Heat a large saucepan on the hob then wash the spinach and put it in the pan. Cover and leave to wilt for 2 minutes, then stir well and drain in a sieve.
- Heat the oil in a large wok and fry the garlic and chilli for 30 seconds.
- Add the squid rings and cook for 1 minute or until they just turn opaque then stir in the spinach, lemon and soy. Serve immediately.

### Stir-fried Squid with Oyster Sauce

**310**

- Omit the spinach and replace the soy sauce with 3 tbsp of oyster sauce.

**311**

**SERVES 4**

# Pork with Mushrooms and Cream

### Creamy Pork Tagliatelle

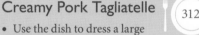

**312**

- Use the dish to dress a large bowl of tagliatelle.

### Pork with Mushrooms and Spinach

**313**

- Add 100 g / 3 ½ oz / 3 ¼ cups baby spinach leaves with the cream and cook until wilted.

PREPARATION TIME 5 MINUTES

COOKING TIME 20 MINUTES

·····································

## INGREDIENTS

2 tbsp olive oil
450 g / 1 lb / 3 cups pork fillet, cubed
200 g / 7 oz / 2 cups mushrooms, sliced
1 tbsp butter
100 ml / 3 ½ fl. oz / ½ cup white wine
200 ml / 7 fl. oz / ¾ cup double (heavy) cream
1 tbsp chives, chopped
salt and pepper

- Heat the oil in a large sauté pan and stir-fry the pork for 5 minutes or until nicely browned. Remove from the pan with a slotted spoon and reserve.
- Add the mushrooms to the pan with the butter and a pinch of salt and fry for 10 minutes or until any liquid that comes out of them has evaporated and they start to colour.
- Add the wine and bubble for 2 minutes then return the pork to the pan.
- Stir in the cream and chives and season with freshly ground black pepper, then bubble for 2 more minutes.

**314**

**SERVES 2**

# Stir-fried Pork and Pineapple

PREPARATION TIME 5 MINUTES

COOKING TIME 8 MINUTES

### INGREDIENTS

3 tbsp vegetable oil
2 cloves garlic, finely chopped
1 tbsp root ginger, finely chopped
225 g / 8 oz / 1 ½ cups pork belly, cubed
300 g / 10 ½ oz / 1 ½ cups canned pineapple rings, drained and halved
2 tbsp rice wine (mirin) or dry sherry
1 tsp caster (superfine) sugar
1 tbsp light soy sauce
a small bunch of chives, cut into short lengths

- Heat the oil in a large wok and fry the garlic and ginger for 30 seconds.
- Add the pork and stir-fry for 2 minutes then add the pineapple and stir-fry for another 2 minutes.
- Mix the rice wine, sugar and soy together and add it to the wok.
- Stir-fry for 2 more minutes then serve immediately, garnished with chives

## Stir-fried Pork and Mandarin

 **315**

- Replace the canned pineapple with canned mandarin segments, drained of the juice.

**316**

**SERVES 4**

# Chicken, Noodle and Broccoli Stir-fry

PREPARATION TIME 5 MINUTES

COOKING TIME 12 MINUTES

### INGREDIENTS

200 g / 7 oz / 2 cups thin egg noodles
½ head broccoli, broken into florets
3 tbsp vegetable oil
2 cloves of garlic, thinly sliced
1 tbsp root ginger, thinly sliced
2 shallots, sliced
4 chestnut mushrooms, thinly sliced
200 g / 7 oz / 1 ¼ cups chicken breast, thinly sliced
2 tbsp light soy sauce
lemon slices to garnish

- Cook the noodles in boiling salted water according to the packet instructions or until al dente, then drain well.
- Meanwhile, blanch the broccoli for 4 minutes then plunge into cold water and drain well.
- Heat the oil in a large wok and fry the garlic, ginger, shallots and mushrooms for 2 minutes.
- Add the chicken and stir-fry for 3 minutes or until just cooked through.
- Add the soy sauce, noodles and broccoli and stir-fry for 2 more minutes.
- Serve immediately, garnished with lemon slices.

## Spicy Chicken Noodle Stir-fry

 **317**

- Add 2 finely chopped red chillies (chilies) and 1 tsp of crushed Szechuan peppercorns to the frying onions.

318

**SERVES 2**

# Stir-fried Prawns and Pineapple

- Heat the oil in a large wok and fry the garlic and ginger for 30 seconds.
- Add the prawns and pineapple and stir-fry for 2 minutes or until the prawns turn opaque.
- Mix the rice wine, sugar and soy together and add it to the wok.
- Stir-fry for 2 more minutes then serve immediately, garnished with chives

PREPARATION TIME 5 MINUTES

COOKING TIME 5 MINUTES

.........................................................

**INGREDIENTS**

3 tbsp vegetable oil
2 cloves of garlic, thinly sliced
1 tbsp root ginger, thinly sliced
200 g / 7 oz / 1 cup raw prawns
(shrimp), peeled with tails left intact
300 g / 10 ½ oz / 1 ½ cups canned
pineapple rings, drained and halved
2 tbsp rice wine (mirin) or dry sherry
1 tsp caster (superfine) sugar
1 tbsp light soy sauce
a small bunch of chives, cut into
short lengths

## Prawns with Pineapple and Chicken

319

- Slice a chicken breast into thin strips and add to the wok along with the garlic. Once cooked through, add the prawns.

---

320

**SERVES 4**

# Stir-fried Beef with Peppers

- Heat the oil in a large wok and fry the garlic and ginger for 30 seconds.
- Add the steak, peppers and spring onions and stir-fry for 4 minutes or until the beef is cooked through.
- Mix the rice wine, sugar and soy together and add it to the wok.
- Stir-fry for 2 more minutes then serve immediately, garnished with coriander (cilantro).

PREPARATION TIME 5 MINUTES

COOKING TIME 8 MINUTES

.........................................................

**INGREDIENTS**

3 tbsp vegetable oil
2 cloves garlic, finely chopped
1 tbsp root ginger, finely chopped
300 g / 10 ½ oz / 2 cups sirloin steak,
sliced
1 yellow pepper, deseeded and sliced
1 green pepper, deseeded and sliced
4 spring onions (scallions), chopped
2 tbsp rice wine (mirin) or dry sherry
1 tsp caster (superfine) sugar
1 tbsp light soy sauce
coriander (cilantro) leaves to garnish

## Stir-fried Beef with Red Peppers

321

- Replace the green and yellow peppers with red peppers and add a handful of bean sprouts in place of the spring onions. Garnish with holy basil instead of coriander (cilantro).

# 322

**SERVES 4**

# Stir-fried Beef with Winter Vegetables

PREPARATION TIME 5 MINUTES

COOKING TIME 10 MINUTES

...............................................

### INGREDIENTS

½ head broccoli, broken into florets
½ cauliflower, broken into florets
2 carrots, cut into batons
100 g / 3 ½ oz / ¾ cup green beans
3 tbsp vegetable oil
2 cloves of garlic, thinly sliced
1 tbsp root ginger, thinly sliced
200 g / 7 oz / 1 ¼ cups sirloin steak,
thinly sliced
2 tbsp light soy sauce
chives to garnish

- Blanch the vegetables for 4 minutes then plunge into cold water and drain well.
- Heat the oil in a large wok and fry the garlic and ginger for 30 seconds.
- Add the beef and stir-fry for 3 minutes or until just cooked through.
- Add the soy sauce and vegetables and stir-fry for 2 more minutes.
- Serve immediately, garnished with chives.

### Beef and Vegetables in Oyster Sauce

323

- Replace the soy sauce with 3 tbsp of oyster sauce mixed with an equal quantity of water.

# 324

**SERVES 4**

# Pork with Coconut, Lime and Paprika

PREPARATION TIME 35 MINUTES

COOKING TIME 8 MINUTES

...............................................

### INGREDIENTS

1 clove of garlic, crushed
1 tsp root ginger, grated
½ tsp paprika
1 lime, juiced and zest finely grated
400 g / 14 oz / 2 ½ cups pork
shoulder, cubed
2 tbsp cornflour (cornstarch)
2 tbsp vegetable oil
200 ml / 7 fl. oz / ¾ cup coconut milk
paprika, lime slices and holy basil
to garnish

- Mix the garlic, ginger and paprika with the lime juice and zest and massage it into the pork.
- Leave to marinate for 30 minutes.
- Pat the pork dry with kitchen paper and dust it with cornflour.
- Heat the oil in a wok and stir-fry the pork over a high heat for 4 minutes or until golden brown and cooked through.
- Pour in the coconut milk and bubble until reduced and thick.
- Spoon onto a serving plate and sprinkle with paprika. Garnish with lime and holy basil.

### Chicken with Coconut, Lime and Paprika

325

- Replace the pork with pieces of boneless, skinless chicken thigh.

326

SERVES 4

# Beef and Noodle Stir-fry

## Egg Fried Noodles

327

- Replace the beef with 2 beaten eggs. Stir-fry until scrambled.

## Crispy Lamb Noodles

328

- Shred 200 g / 7 oz / 1 ¼ cups of leftover roast lamb and deep fry at 190°C until crisp, then add it to the noodles in place of the beef.

PREPARATION TIME 5 MINUTES

COOKING TIME 10 MINUTES

### INGREDIENTS

200 g / 7 oz / 2 cups thin egg noodles
3 tbsp vegetable oil
2 cloves of garlic, thinly sliced
1 tbsp root ginger, thinly sliced
2 small dried chillies (chilies)
200 g / 7 oz / 1 ¼ cups sirloin steak, thinly sliced
2 tbsp light soy sauce
2 tbsp peanuts, roughly chopped
2 tbsp mint leaves
2 tbsp coriander (cilantro) leaves

- Cook the noodles in boiling salted water according to the packet instructions or until al dente, then drain well.
- Heat the oil in a large wok and fry the garlic, ginger, and dried chillies for 30 seconds.
- Add the beef and stir-fry for 3 minutes or until just cooked through.
- Add the soy sauce, noodles and peanuts and stir-fry for 2 more minutes.
- Serve immediately, garnished with herbs.

329

SERVES 4

# Lamb and Shrimp Biryani

PREPARATION TIME 5 MINUTES

COOKING TIME 30 MINUTES

## INGREDIENTS

2 tbsp vegetable oil
1 onion, finely chopped
2 cloves of garlic, finely chopped
2 tsp root ginger, grated
2 lamb neck fillets, sliced
1 tbsp mild curry powder
200 g / 7 oz / 1 cup long grain rice
4 tbsp coriander (cilantro) leaves,
roughly chopped
400 ml / 14 fl. oz / 1 ⅔ cups vegetable
stock
100 g / 3 ½ oz / ¾ cup cooked brown
shrimps
1 lime, juiced
red onion slices to garnish

- Heat the oil in a large saucepan and fry the onion, garlic and ginger for 2 minutes.
- Add the lamb and stir-fry until it starts to colour then stir in the curry powder and a pinch of salt.
- Stir in the rice and half the coriander and cook for 1 minute.
- Pour in enough stock to cover the rice by 1 cm (½ in) and bring to the boil.
- Put the lid on and turn the heat down to its lowest setting.
- Cook the rice for 10 minutes then turn off the heat and leave to stand for 10 minutes without removing the lid.
- Stir in the brown shrimps, lime juice and the rest of the coriander then divide between 4 warm bowls and garnish with onion slices.

## Lamb and Apricot Biryani

330

- Replace the shrimps with an equal weight of chopped dried apricots.

331

SERVES 4

# Chicken and Mango Stir-fry

PREPARATION TIME 5 MINUTES

COOKING TIME 8 MINUTES

## INGREDIENTS

3 tbsp vegetable oil
2 cloves garlic, finely chopped
1 tbsp root ginger, finely chopped
1 red chilli (chili), halved and sliced
200 g / 7 oz / 1 ¼ cups chicken breast,
sliced
1 carrot, julienned
1 mango, peeled, stoned and cut
into strips
2 tbsp rice wine or dry sherry
2 tbsp runny honey
1 tbsp light soy sauce

- Heat the oil in a large wok and fry the garlic, ginger and chilli for 30 seconds.
- Add the chicken and carrot and stir-fry for 2 minutes then add the mango and stir-fry for another 2 minutes.
- Mix the rice wine with the honey and soy and add it to the wok.
- Stir-fry for 2 more minutes then serve immediately.

## Monkfish and Mango Stir-fry

332

- Replace the chicken with an equal weight of monkfish, cut into chunks.

## 333

**SERVES 4**

# Mussels with Chilli and Lemongrass

- Heat the oil in a wok and fry the garlic, chilli, lemongrass and curry paste for 2 minutes.
- Add the mussels, stock and sugar to the pan and put on the lid.
- Cook for 5 minutes or until the mussels have steamed open. Discard any that have remained closed.
- Stir in the lime juice and chives and serve immediately.

PREPARATION TIME 2 MINUTES

COOKING TIME 8 MINUTES

### INGREDIENTS

2 tbsp vegetable oil
1 clove of garlic, skin on
1 red chilli (chili), halved and thinly sliced
1 lemongrass stem, thinly sliced
1 tbsp Thai yellow curry paste
900 g / 2 lb / 4 ½ cups live mussels, cleaned
400 ml / 14 fl. oz / 1 ⅔ cups fish stock
1 tsp caster (superfine) sugar
1 lime, juiced
1 tbsp chives, chopped

### Mussels with Ginger and Coconut 334

- Replace the lemongrass with 1 tbsp of thinly sliced root ginger and use coconut milk instead of the fish stock.

## 335

**SERVES 4**

# Kumquat-marinated Chicken Thigh

- Put all of the ingredients except the chicken into a food processor and blend to a puree.
- Spread the mixture over the skin of the chicken thighs and leave to marinate for 30 minutes.
- Preheat the grill to its highest setting.
- Grill the chicken thighs for 8 minutes, turning half way through until cooked through and golden.

PREPARATION TIME 35 MINUTES

COOKING TIME 8 MINUTES

### INGREDIENTS

8 kumquats
2 tbsp honey
2 tbsp dark soy sauce
1 clove of garlic, crushed
1 tbsp root ginger, grated
1 tsp sesame oil
4 boneless chicken thighs

### Kumquat-marinated Pork Belly 336

- Use the marinade to flavour a 600 g / 1 lb 4 oz / 3 ¾ cups piece of pork belly and roast at 220°C for 40 minutes.

337

**SERVES 4**

# Barbecue Pork Belly

### Barbecue Chicken Wings

338

- Use the marinade to coat 12 chicken wings and reduce the cooking time to 20 minutes.

### Barbecue Spare Ribs

339

- Gently poach 1 kg / 2 lb 2 oz / 6 cups of spare ribs in chicken stock for 30 minutes, then drain and dry with kitchen towel before brushing with the marinade and barbecuing.

PREPARATION TIME 40 MINUTES

COOKING TIME 25 MINUTES

..........................................................

### INGREDIENTS

½ onion, finely grated
2 cloves garlic, crushed
2 tbsp soy sauce
1 tbsp tomato ketchup
1 tbsp dark brown sugar
1 tsp Worcestershire sauce
1 tsp Chinese five spice powder
800 g / 1 lb 12 oz / 5 cups boneless pork belly, skin removed

- Mix the onion, garlic, soy, ketchup, sugar, Worcestershire sauce and five spice together and massage it into the pork. Leave to marinate for 20 minutes.
- Prepare a barbecue or preheat the grill to its highest setting.
- Grill or barbecue the pork for 25 minutes, turning and basting occasionally, until the meat is cooked through and tender.
- Cut into slices and serve hot or at room temperature.

**340**

**SERVES 4**

# Chicken with Asparagus and Holy Basil

- Heat the oil in a wok and fry the curry paste for 1 minute.
- Add the chicken and asparagus and stir-fry for 2 minutes, then add the red pepper and stir-fry for 4 minutes.
- Pour in the coconut milk and bubble until reduced almost to nothing.
- Stir in the spring onions and holy basil and serve immediately.

PREPARATION TIME 2 MINUTES

COOKING TIME 10 MINUTES

...................................................

**INGREDIENTS**

1 tbsp vegetable oil
1 tbsp Thai green curry paste
400 g / 14 oz / 2 cups chicken breast, sliced
400 g / 14 oz / 4 cups asparagus tips
½ red pepper, deseeded and sliced
100 ml / 3 ½ fl. oz / ½ cup coconut milk
2 spring onions (scallions), thinly sliced
a small bunch holy basil, leaves only

## Prawns with Asparagus and Holy Basil

**341**

- Replace the chicken with 200 g / 7 oz / 1 cup of peeled prawns, adding them at the red pepper stage.

**342**

**SERVES 4**

# Chicken Satay

- Put 12 wooden skewers in a bowl of water and leave to soak for 20 minutes.
- Meanwhile, mix together the peanut butter, honey, soy, spice and garlic and massage it into the chicken pieces.
- Leave to marinate for 20 minutes.
- Preheat the grill to its highest setting.
- Thread the chicken onto the skewers then cook them under the grill for 4 minutes on each side or until they are golden brown and cooked through.
- Serve with red onion marmalade.

PREPARATION TIME 30 MINUTES

COOKING TIME 8 MINUTES

...................................................

**INGREDIENTS**

4 tbsp crunchy peanut butter
1 tbsp runny honey
2 tbsp dark soy sauce
1 tsp Chinese five spice powder
1 clove of garlic, crushed
6 skinless chicken breasts, cubed
red onion marmalade to serve

## Tofu Satay

**343**

- Replace the chicken with 600 g / 1 lb 3 oz / 2 ½ cups of firm tofu cubes.

**344**

**SERVES 4**

# Stir-fried Vegetables

PREPARATION TIME 2 MINUTES

COOKING TIME 6 MINUTES

## INGREDIENTS

2 tbsp vegetable oil
2 cloves garlic, finely chopped
1 tbsp root ginger, finely chopped
1 fennel bulb, thinly sliced
½ Chinese cabbage, shredded
1 courgette (zucchini), diced
1 red pepper, deseeded and julienned
2 tomatoes, cut into wedges
2 tbsp rice wine (mirin) or dry sherry
1 tsp caster (superfine) sugar
1 tbsp light soy sauce

- Heat the oil in a large wok and fry the garlic and ginger for 30 seconds.
- Add the vegetables and stir-fry for 4 minutes.
- Mix the rice wine, sugar and soy together and add it to the wok.
- Stir-fry for 1 more minute then serve immediately.

### Stir-steamed Vegetables

**345**

- For a fat-free version of this dish, use water instead of oil at the beginning, adding extra splashes of water whenever the vegetables get too dry.

**346**

**SERVES 4**

# Chicken, Noodle and Shiitake Stir-fry

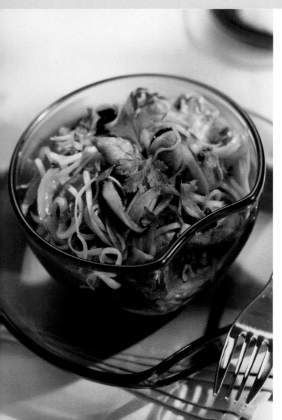

PREPARATION TIME 5 MINUTES

COOKING TIME 15 MINUTES

## INGREDIENTS

200 g / 7 oz / 2 cups Pho or Pad Thai rice noodles
3 tbsp vegetable oil
2 cloves of garlic, thinly sliced
1 tbsp root ginger, thinly sliced
2 shallots, sliced
100 g / 3 ½ oz / 1 cup shiitake mushrooms, thinly sliced
200 g / 7 oz / 1 ¼ cups chicken breast, thinly sliced
2 tbsp light soy sauce
chopped coriander (cilantro) to garnish

- Cook the noodles in boiling salted water according to the packet instructions or until al dente, then drain well.
- Heat the oil in a large wok and fry the garlic, ginger, shallots and mushrooms for 2 minutes.
- Add the chicken and stir-fry for 3 minutes or until just cooked through.
- Add the soy sauce and noodles and stir-fry for 2 more minutes.
- Serve immediately, garnished with coriander.

### Chicken and Shiitake Fried Rice

**347**

- Replace the cooked noodles with cooked long grain rice.

# Chicken and Pea Thai Green Curry

**348**

**SERVES 4**

- Heat the oil in a wok and fry the curry paste and shallots for 2 minutes.
- Add the chicken to the wok and stir-fry for 4 minutes then add the coconut milk and peas and bring to a simmer.
- Season to taste with the caster sugar and fish sauce before serving in warm bowls, garnished with holy basil.
- Serve with jasmine rice.

PREPARATION TIME 5 MINUTES

COOKING TIME 12 MINUTES

### INGREDIENTS

2 tbsp vegetable oil
2 tbsp Thai green curry paste
2 shallots, chopped
2 skinless chicken breasts, cut into chunks
400 ml / 14 fl. oz / 1 ⅔ cups coconut milk
200 g / 7 oz / 1 ⅓ cup frozen peas, defrosted
1 tsp caster (superfine) sugar
1 tbsp fish sauce
a few sprigs holy basil
jasmine rice to serve

## Chicken and Bamboo Shoot Curry

**349**

- Replace the peas with 200 g / 7 oz / 1 cup of canned bamboo shoots.

# Prawn and Chicken Rice

**350**

**SERVES 4**

- Heat the oil in a large wok and fry the ginger and garlic for 30 seconds.
- Add the chicken and mushrooms and stir-fry for 3 minutes then add the prawns and fry for another 2 minutes.
- Add the rice and stir-fry until piping hot. This should take about 4 minutes.
- Add the soy, sesame oil and coriander and cook for 1 more minute then serve immediately.

PREPARATION TIME 2 MINUTES

COOKING TIME 12 MINUTES

### INGREDIENTS

3 tbsp olive oil
1 tsp root ginger, grated
1 clove of garlic, crushed
200 g / 7 oz / 1 ¼ cups chicken breast, thinly sliced
150 g / 5 ½ oz / 1 ½ cups mushrooms, sliced
150 g / 5 ½ oz / 1 cup raw prawns (shrimp), peeled
300 g / 10 ½ oz / 1 ¾ cup long grain rice, cooked and cooled
2 tbsp light soy sauce
1 tsp sesame oil
a small bunch coriander (cilantro), leaves only

## Fried Rice with Chicken and Mushrooms

**351**

- Omit the prawns and add 3 tbsp of soaked, sliced wood ear fungus when you add the mushrooms.

## 352
**SERVES 4**

# Haddock and Butternut Squash Gratin

PREPARATION TIME 10 MINUTES

COOKING TIME 35 MINUTES

### INGREDIENTS

450 g / 1 lb / 3 cups butternut squash, peeled and cubed
600 ml / 1 pint / 2 ½ cups whole milk
450 g / 1 lb / 2 ¼ cups smoked haddock
3 tbsp butter
1 tbsp plain (all purpose) flour
2 tbsp flat leaf parsley, chopped
15 g / ½ oz breadcrumbs

- Cook the squash in boiling salted water for 12 minutes then drain well.
- Bring the milk to a simmer then pour over the haddock. Cover the dish with film and leave for 10 minutes. Drain off and reserve the milk and flake the haddock, discarding any skin and bones.
- When the squash is ready, mash it until smooth with 1 tablespoon of the butter and a little of the haddock milk.
- Heat 1 tablespoon of the butter in a saucepan and stir in the flour. Gradually incorporate the rest of the haddock milk. Stir until it starts to bubble then stir in the parsley and flaked haddock.
- Preheat the grill to its highest setting. Pour the haddock mixture into a dish and top with the mashed squash.
- Dot 1 tbsp of butter over the top and sprinkle with breadcrumbs then grill for 5 minutes until golden.

### Haddock and Sweet Potato Gratin
 353

- Replace the squash with an equal weight of sweet potato.

## 354
**SERVES 2**

# Rib-eye Steak with Niçoise Vegetables

PREPARATION TIME 8 MINUTES

COOKING TIME 40 MINUTES

### INGREDIENTS

2 rib-eye steaks
2 tbsp olive oil
½ tsp smoked paprika

FOR THE VEGETABLES
200 g / 7 oz / 1 ¼ cups baby new potatoes
200 g / 7 oz / 1 cup vine cherry tomatoes
2 tbsp olive oil
75 g / 2 ½ oz / ½ cup black olives

- Preheat the oven to 200°C (180°C fan) / 390F / gas 6.
- Boil the potatoes in boiling salted water for 12 minutes or until tender. Drain well.
- Arrange the potatoes and tomatoes in a roasting tin, drizzle with oil and season with salt and pepper.
- Roast for 25 minutes, then add the olives and roast for 5 more minutes.
- Meanwhile, brush the steaks with oil and season liberally with salt, pepper and paprika.
- Heat a large frying pan until smoking hot then fry the steaks for 6 minutes, turning them every 2 minutes.
- Transfer the steaks to a warm plate and cover with foil, then leave to rest for 5 minutes.
- Divide the steaks and vegetables between 2 warm plates and serve immediately.

### Lamb Chops with Niçoise Vegetables
355

- Replace the steaks with 3 lamb chops per person.

**356**

**SERVES 2**

# Baked Chicken with Vegetables

## Lemon Baked Chicken

**357**

- Replace the lime juice and slices with lemon.

## Orange Baked Chicken

**358**

- Replace the lime juice and slices with orange.

PREPARATION TIME 10 MINUTES

COOKING TIME 35 MINUTES

### INGREDIENTS

1 lime, juiced
1 tsp runny honey
2 chicken breasts
1 large tomato, halved
1 courgette (zucchini), sliced
3 tbsp olive oil
2 tbsp breadcrumbs
1 tsp flat leaf parsley, finely chopped
lime slices and parsley to garnish

- Mix the lime juice with the honey and a pinch of salt and pour it over the chicken. Leave to marinate for 10 minutes.
- Preheat the oven to 200°C (180°C fan) / 390F, /gas 6.
- Drizzle the oil over the tomato, courgette and chicken.
- Arrange them in a baking dish and season well with salt and pepper.
- Bake for 25 minutes then stack up the courgette slices and sprinkle the tomatoes and courgette stack with breadcrumbs and parsley.
- Return to the oven for 10 minutes or until the chicken is cooked through.
- Garnish the chicken with lime slices and parsley before serving.

**359**

**SERVES 2**

# Pork Chops with Potatoes

PREPARATION TIME 10 MINUTES

COOKING TIME 20 MINUTES

### INGREDIENTS

10 new potatoes, halved
2 woody sprigs of rosemary
2 pork chops
4 tbsp olive oil
salt and pepper
2 tbsp thyme leaves
2 courgettes (zucchini)

- Boil the potatoes in salted water for 12 minutes or until tender. Drain well.
- Meanwhile, preheat the grill to its highest setting and put a griddle pan on the hob to heat.
- Strip most of the leaves off the rosemary sprigs and thread the potatoes onto the woody stems like a skewer.
- Brush the pork and potatoes with half the oil and season with salt, pepper and thyme leaves.
- Grill for 4 minutes on each side, or until the pork is cooked through.
- Meanwhile, cut the courgettes into thin ribbons with a vegetable peeler and brush them with oil.
- Griddle the ribbons for 2 minutes on each side or until nicely marked.
- Divide the pork, potatoes and courgettes between 2 warm plates and serve immediately.

## Potato and Mushroom Rosemary Skewers

 **360**

- Halve the quantity of potatoes and thread alternately onto the rosemary skewers with whole chestnut mushrooms.

**361**

**SERVES 4**

# Tofu and Vegetable Kebabs

PREPARATION TIME 30 MINUTES

COOKING TIME 8 MINUTES

### INGREDIENTS

1 tbsp dried herbes de Provence
3 tbsp olive oil
400 g / 14 oz / 2 ½ cups firm tofu, cubed
1 yellow pepper, deseeded and cubed
1 large courgette (zucchini), quartered and sliced
12 cherry tomatoes

- Put 12 wooden skewers in a bowl of water and leave to soak for 20 minutes.
- Meanwhile, stir the herbs into the oil and toss with the tofu and vegetables.
- Leave to marinate for 20 minutes.
- Preheat the grill to its highest setting.
- Thread the tofu and vegetables onto the skewers and spread them out on a large grill tray.
- Grill the kebabs for 4 minutes on each side or until they are golden brown and cooked through.

## Tofu and Pineapple Kebabs

 **362**

- Replace the courgette (zucchini) with chunks of fresh pineapple.

**363**

**SERVES 2**

# Steak with Balsamic Peppers and Crisps

- Mix the balsamic vinegar with the honey and stir it into the peppers. Leave to marinate for 10 minutes.
- Preheat the oven to 200°C (180°C fan) / 390F / gas 6.
- Rinse the potatoes under cold water then dry well.
- Rub the potatoes with oil and season then spread them out on a large non-stick baking tray.
- Crisp the potatoes in the oven for 15 minutes, turning half way through. Meanwhile, preheat a griddle pan until smoking hot.
- Brush the steaks with the oil and season well. Griddle the steaks for 4 minutes then turn them over and cook for another 4 minutes.
- Transfer the steaks to a warm plate, wrap in foil, and leave to rest for 5 minutes.
- Transfer the steaks to warm plates and spoon over the peppers. Top with rocket and serve crisps on the side.

PREPARATION TIME 12 MINUTES

COOKING TIME 15 MINUTES

.........................................................

### INGREDIENTS

2 tbsp balsamic vinegar
2 tsp runny honey
1 jar roasted red peppers in oil, drained
2 small sirloin steaks
1 tbsp olive oil
a handful rocket (arugula) leaves

FOR THE POTATOES
2 maris piper potatoes, peeled and very thinly sliced
4 tbsp olive oil
salt and pepper

### Pan-fried Cod with Griddled Peppers

**364**

- Use the balsamic peppers and rocket (arugula) to dress 2 portions of pan-fried cod fillet.

**365**

**SERVES 4**

# Grilled Belly Pork with Honey and Lime

- Squeeze the lime quarters into a bowl and put them on one side.
- Stir the honey, soy and five spice into the lime juice then pour it over the pork steaks and empty lime quarters. Leave to marinate for 25 minutes.
- Preheat the grill to its highest setting.
- Arrange the pork belly and lime on a large grill tray and grill for 4 minutes on each side or until the glaze is golden and sticky and the pork is cooked through.
- Serve with steamed jasmine rice.

PREPARATION TIME 30 MINUTES

COOKING TIME 8 MINUTES

.........................................................

### INGREDIENTS

2 limes, quartered
2 tbsp runny honey
2 tbsp dark soy sauce
½ tsp Chinese 5 spice powder
4 pork belly steaks, skin removed
jasmine rice to serve

### Grilled Liver with Honey and Lime

**366**

- Replace the pork belly with strips of pork liver and reduce the cooking time to 2 minutes on each side.

367

**SERVES 4**

# Grilled Salmon with Honey and Lime

### Grilled Prawns with Honey and Lime

368

- Replace the salmon with raw king prawns (shrimp) and reduce the cooking time to 1 minute on each side.

### Grilled Tuna with Honey and Lime

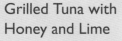
369

- Substitute the salmon with fresh tuna steaks and reduce the cooking time to 2 minutes on each side.

PREPARATION TIME 30 MINUTES

COOKING TIME 6 MINUTES

### INGREDIENTS

2 tbsp runny honey
2 tbsp light soy sauce
2 limes, sliced
4 portions salmon fillet, skinned

- Mix the honey with the soy and stir in the limes then pour it over the salmon. Leave to marinate for 25 minutes.
- Preheat the grill to its highest setting.
- Arrange the salmon and lime slices on a large grill tray and grill for 3 minutes on each side or until the glaze is golden and sticky and the salmon is just cooked in the centre.

## 370

**SERVES 4**

# Honey and Orange Spare Rib Chops

- Stir together the orange juice, honey and soy and pour it over the spare rib chops. Leave to marinate for 25 minutes.
- Meanwhile, boil the potatoes in salted water for 12 minutes or until tender then drain well.
- Preheat the grill to its highest setting and heat a griddle pan until smoking hot.
- Mix the oil with the rosemary and rub it into the potatoes and baby corn.
- Grill the pork for 4 minutes on each side or until the glaze is golden and sticky and the pork is cooked through.
- While the pork is cooking, griddle the potatoes and baby corn for 8 minutes, turning once.
- Divide the pork and vegetables between 4 warm plates and serve immediately.

PREPARATION TIME 20 MINUTES

COOKING TIME 8 MINUTES

### INGREDIENTS

1 orange, juiced
2 tbsp runny honey
2 tbsp light soy sauce
8 pork spare rib chops

### FOR THE GRIDDLED VEGETABLES

400 g / 14 oz / 2 ¼ cups new potatoes, halved
2 tbsp olive oil
2 tsp fresh rosemary, chopped
8 baby sweetcorn

### Honey and Orange Duck Breasts

## 371

- Replace the spare rib chops with 1 small duck breast per person.

## 372

**SERVES 2**

# Grilled Swordfish with Sprouting Seeds

- Mix together the dressing ingredients and pour them over the shallots. Leave to macerate for 20 minutes.
- Preheat the grill to its highest setting.
- Brush the swordfish with oil then grill it for 3 minutes on each side or until cooked to your liking.
- Transfer the fish to 2 warm plates and spoon over the dressing, then garnish with the sprouts and chives.

PREPARATION TIME 25 MINUTES

COOKING TIME 6 MINUTES

### INGREDIENTS

2 swordfish steaks
2 tbsp olive oil
50 g / 1 ¾ oz / 1 cup alfalfa sprouts
50 g / 1 ¾ oz / ½ cup bean sprouts
4 chives

### FOR THE DRESSING

2 tbsp soy sauce
1 tbsp rice wine (mirin)
½ tsp caster (superfine) sugar
1 tsp sesame oil
a pinch chilli (chili) powder
½ tsp Szechuan peppercorns, crushed
4 small shallots, peeled

### Grilled Tuna with Sprouting Seeds

## 373

- Replace the swordfish with fresh tuna steaks.

**374**

**SERVES 4**

# Penne Salad with Goats' Cheese

**PREPARATION TIME 5 MINUTES**

**COOKING TIME 12 MINUTES**

## INGREDIENTS

400 g / 14 oz / 4 cups penne
100 g / 3 ½ oz / ¾ cup fresh peas
8 tomatoes, cut into wedges
4 slices prosciutto, chopped
100 g / 3 ½ oz / ⅔ cup goats' cheese,
crumbled
a small bunch basil, leaves only
4 tbsp extra virgin olive oil

- Cook the penne in boiling salted water according to the packet instructions or until al dente.
- 4 minutes before the end of cooking time, add the peas to the pot.
- Drain the pasta and peas and toss with the tomato, prosciutto, goats' cheese and basil.
- Dress the salad with olive oil and serve warm or at room temperature.

## Penne Salad with Stilton and Chorizo

**375**

- Replace the goats' cheese with Stilton and the Parma ham with chorizo.

**376**

**SERVES 2**

# Tagliatelle a la Carbonara

**PREPARATION TIME 5 MINUTES**

**COOKING TIME 14 MINUTES**

## INGREDIENTS

200 g / 7 oz / 2 cups tagliatelle
100 g / 3 ½ oz / ¾ cup guanciale or
pancetta, thinly sliced
3 cloves of garlic, crushed
4 tbsp olive oil
50 g / 1 ¾ oz / ½ cup Parmesan,
finely grated
1 egg, beaten

- Cook the tagliatelle in boiling salted water according to the packet instructions or until al dente.
- Meanwhile, fry the meat strips and garlic in the oil for 2 minutes or until golden brown.
- Stir the Parmesan into the beaten egg.
- Reserve 1 ladleful of the pasta cooking water and drain the rest.
- Return the pasta to the pan and add the pancetta and Parmesan mixtures. Stir well and add enough of the pasta water to make a thick sauce.
- Divide the pasta between 2 warm bowls and sprinkle with freshly ground black pepper.

## Mushroom Carbonara

**377**

- Finely slice 6 closed cup mushrooms and add to the pancetta.

**378**

SERVES 4

# Pork and Brie Roulades

- Preheat the oven to 200°C (180°C fan) / 390F / gas 6
- Put the pork between 2 sheets of clingfilm and bash it flat with a rolling pin. Peel off the clingfilm.
- Lay the prosciutto slices out on a chopping board and top with the basil leaves.
- Top each one with a piece of pork then lay the Brie on top.
- Roll them up into roulades and secure with a skewer or cocktail stick.
- Transfer the roulades to a roasting tin and cook in the oven for 25–30 minutes or until the pork is cooked in the centre.
- Serve with spaghetti or a green salad.

PREPARATION TIME 15 MINUTES

COOKING TIME 25–30 MINUTES

### INGREDIENTS

4 pork escalopes
4 slices prosciutto
12 large basil leaves
8 slices Brie

### Rose Veal and Brie Roulades

 **379**

- Replace the pork with rose veal.

 **380**

SERVES 4

# Penne with Broccoli and Garlic

- Cook the garlic cloves in a large saucepan of boiling salted water for 15 minutes.
- Add the penne to the pan and cook according to the packet instructions or until al dente.
- 4 minutes before the end of cooking time, add the broccoli to the pan.
- Reserve 1 ladle of the cooking water and drain the rest then toss the penne, broccoli and garlic cloves with the oil and season with salt and pepper.
- If the pasta looks a bit dry, add a little of the cooking water and shake the pan to emulsify.
- Divide the pasta between 4 warm bowls and use a vegetable peeler to shave over some Parmesan.
- The softened garlic can be squeezed out of the skins at the table and eaten with the pasta.

PREPARATION TIME 5 MINUTES

COOKING TIME 30 MINUTES

### INGREDIENTS

1 bulb of garlic, cloves separated
400 g / 14 oz / 4 cups penne
1 small head broccoli, broken into florets
6 tbsp olive oil
salt and pepper
30 g / 1 oz / ¼ cup Parmesan

### Penne with Broccoli and Garlic Sauce

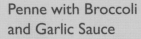 **381**

- Cook pasta separately. When the garlic is cooked, squeeze it out of its skins into a food processor and blend with the broccoli and oil. Season well.

382

SERVES 1

# Clam Omelette

## Mussel Omelette

383

- Replace the clams with cooked, shelled mussels.

## Sweetcorn Omelette

384

- Replace the clams with 100 g / 3 ½ oz / ⅔ cup of canned sweetcorn.

PREPARATION TIME 3 MINUTES

COOKING TIME 4 MINUTES

### INGREDIENTS

3 large eggs
salt and pepper
1 tbsp butter
50 g / 1 ¾ oz / ¼ cup cooked shelled clams
1 tbsp flat leaf parsley, finely chopped

- Break the eggs into a jug with a pinch of salt and pepper and beat them gently to break up the yolks.
- Heat the butter in a non-stick frying pan until sizzling then pour in the eggs.
- Cook over a medium heat until the eggs start to set around the outside. Use a spatula to draw the sides of the omelette into the centre and tilt the pan to fill the gaps with more liquid egg.
- Repeat the process until the top of the omelette is just set then sprinkle over the clams and parsley.
- Shake the omelette out onto a plate, folding it over as you go.

## 385

SERVES 1

# Tofu and Spring Onion Omelette

- Break the eggs into a jug with a pinch of salt and pepper and beat them gently to break up the yolks.
- Stir in the tofu and spring onions.
- Heat the butter in a non-stick frying pan until sizzling then pour in the eggs.
- Cook over a medium heat until the eggs start to set around the outside. Use a spatula to draw the sides of the omelette into the centre and tilt the pan to fill the gaps with more liquid egg.
- Repeat the process until the top of the omelette is just set then fold in half and sprinkle over the parsley.

PREPARATION TIME 3 MINUTES

COOKING TIME 4 MINUTES

**INGREDIENTS**

3 large eggs
salt and pepper
2 tbsp flat leaf parsley, chopped
1 tbsp butter
50 g / 1 ¾ oz / ¼ cup firm tofu, cubed
2 spring onions (scallions), chopped
flat leaf parsley to garnish

### Halloumi and Spring Onion Omelette

## 386

- Replace the tofu with cubes of Halloumi.

## 387

SERVES 6

# Savoury Tomato and Pesto Crumble

- Preheat the oven to 180°C (160°C fan) / 355F / gas 4.
- Arrange the tomatoes in a baking dish and spread the pesto on top.
- Rub the butter into the flour and stir in the ground almonds, then season with salt and pepper.
- Take a handful of the topping and squeeze it into a clump, then crumble it over the vegetables.
- Repeat with the rest of the crumble mixture then press down with your fingertips into an even layer. Bake the crumble for 40 minutes or until the topping is golden brown.

PREPARATION TIME 8 MINUTES

COOKING TIME 40 MINUTES

**INGREDIENTS**

400 g / 14 oz / 2 cups canned tomatoes, drained
4 tbsp pesto
75 g / 2 ½ oz / ⅓ cup butter
50 g / 1 ¾ oz / ⅓ cup plain (all purpose) flour
25 g / 1 oz / ¼ cup ground almonds
salt and pepper

### Tomato and Tapenade Crumble

## 388

- Replace the pesto with black olive tapenade.

**389**

**SERVES 4**

# Chicken and Red Onion Pasta Bake

PREPARATION TIME 5 MINUTES

COOKING TIME 25 MINUTES

## INGREDIENTS

400 g / 14 oz / 4 cups cavatappi pasta
4 tbsp olive oil
1 red onion, sliced
200 g / 7 oz / 1 ¼ cups chicken breast, sliced
2 tbsp flat leaf parsley, finely chopped
300 ml / 10 ½ fl. oz / 1 ¼ cups white wine
150 g / 5 ½ oz / 1 ½ cups mozzarella, cubed

- Preheat the oven to 220°C (200°C fan) / 430F / gas 7.
- Cook the cavatappi in boiling salted water according to the packet instructions or until al dente. Drain well.
- Meanwhile, heat the oil in a frying pan and cook the onions with a pinch of salt for 5 minutes.
- Add the chicken and stir-fry for 3 minutes then sprinkle with parsley, pour in the wine, and bring to a simmer.
- Stir in the pasta and spoon it into a baking dish.
- Level the top and scatter over the mozzarella cubes then bake for 10 minutes or until the top is bubbling.

### Chicken and Mushroom Pasta Bake

**390**

- Add 100 g / 3 ½ oz / ½ cup of sliced button mushrooms when you fry the chicken.

**391**

**SERVES 4**

# Chicken and Red Onion Hot Pot

PREPARATION TIME 8 MINUTES

COOKING TIME 45 MINUTES

## INGREDIENTS

400 g / 14 oz / 2 ¼ cups maris piper potatoes, peeled and sliced
4 tbsp olive oil
1 red onion, sliced
200 g / 7 oz / 1 ¼ cups chicken breast, sliced
2 tsp Dijon mustard
300 ml / 10 ½ fl. oz / 1 ¼ cups white wine
50 g / 1 ¾ oz / ¼ cup butter, melted
salt and pepper

- Preheat the oven to 220°C (200°C fan) / 430F / gas 7 and put a baking dish in to heat.
- Cook the potatoes in boiling salted water for 10 minutes or until tender. Drain well.
- Meanwhile, heat the oil in a frying pan and cook the onions with a pinch of salt for 5 minutes.
- Add the chicken and stir-fry for 3 minutes then stir in the mustard, pour in the wine, and bring to a simmer.
- Spoon the chicken mixture into the preheated baking dish and arrange the potatoes on top.
- Brush the potatoes with melted butter and sprinkle with salt and pepper, then bake for 30 minutes or until the potatoes are golden.

### Quick Lamb Hot Pot

**392**

- Replace the chicken with lamb neck fillet, cut into cubes.

393

**SERVES 1**

# Wild Mushroom Omelette

## Mushroom and Bacon Omelette

394

- Add 2 chopped rashers of smoked streaky bacon to the pan with the mushrooms.

## Creamy Mushroom Omelette

395

- Add 2 tbsp of crème fraîche to the mushrooms for the last minute of cooking time.

PREPARATION TIME 10 MINUTES

COOKING TIME 15 MINUTES

### INGREDIENTS

200 g / 8 oz / 2 cups mixed wild mushrooms (to include chanterelles and ceps)
1 tbsp olive oil
4 tbsp butter
salt and pepper
3 large eggs
1 tbsp chives, chopped

- Pick over the mushrooms and brush away any soil with a pastry brush. Cut the bigger mushrooms into bite-sized pieces.
- Heat the olive oil and half the butter in a large sauté pan until sizzling.
- Add the mushrooms, season with salt and pepper and cook for 10 minutes, stirring occasionally.
- Break the eggs into a jug with a pinch of salt and pepper and beat them gently to break up the yolks.
- Heat the rest of the butter in a non-stick frying pan until sizzling then pour in the eggs.
- Cook over a medium heat until the eggs start to set around the outside. Use a spatula to draw the sides of the omelette into the centre and tilt the pan to fill the gaps with more liquid egg.
- Repeat the process until the top of the omelette is just set then fold it over and slide onto a warm plate.
- Spoon over the mushrooms and sprinkle with chives.

**396**

**SERVES 2**

# Ravioli with Tomato, Basil and Pine Nuts

## Ravioli with Mushrooms and Truffle Oil

**397**

- Dress the ravioli with 100 g / 3 ½ oz / 1 cup of sliced mushrooms that have been fried in 1 tbsp of butter. Add a few drops of truffle oil to the pan just before serving.

## Ravioli with Gorgonzola Cream

**398**

- Dress the ravioli with 150 ml / ¼ pt / ⅔ cup double (heavy) cream and 50 g / 2 oz / ¼ cup Gorgonzola that have been heated together.

PREPARATION TIME 2 MINUTES

COOKING TIME 10 MINUTES

### INGREDIENTS

250 g / 9 oz / 2 cups fresh ravioli
2 tbsp pine nuts
6 sun-dried tomatoes in oil, chopped
2 tbsp oil from the sun-dried tomato jar
a small bunch basil, shredded

- Cook the ravioli in boiling salted water according to the packet instructions or until al dente.
- Meanwhile, dry-fry the pine nuts in a frying pan until toasted.
- Take off the heat and stir in the sun-dried tomatoes and their oil.
- Drain the ravioli and split between 2 warm bowls then spoon over the sun-dried tomato mixture and sprinkle with basil.

**399**

**SERVES 4**

# Fried Gnocchi with Tomato Sauce

- Heat the oil for the sauce in a sauté pan and fry the onion for 5 minutes to soften. Add the garlic and cook for 2 more minutes, then stir in the tomatoes. Simmer for 15 minutes.
- Meanwhile, heat the oil in a large non-stick frying pan and fry the gnocchi for 5 minutes, turning once.
- Divide the gnocchi between 4 warm bowls and top with a spoonful of tomato sauce.

PREPARATION TIME 5 MINUTES

COOKING TIME 20 MINUTES

**INGREDIENTS**

4 tbsp olive oil
500 g / 1 lb 2 oz / 2 cups ready-made gnocchi

FOR THE SAUCE
4 tbsp olive oil
1 onion, sliced
2 cloves of garlic, crushed
400 g / 14 oz / 2 cups canned tomatoes, chopped

### Gnocchi with Dolcelatte Cream

 **400**

- Replace the tomato sauce with a sauce of dolcelatte cheese cubes, melted in a small pot of double (heavy) cream.

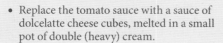

**401**

**SERVES 4**

# Baked Maccheroncini with Pancetta and Mozzarella

- Preheat the oven to 220°C (200°C fan) / 430F / gas 7.
- Cook the maccheroncini in boiling salted water according to the packet instructions or until al dente. Drain well.
- Meanwhile, heat the oil in a frying pan and fry the pancetta for 5 minutes.
- Pour in the wine, bring to a simmer and cook for 5 minutes.
- Stir in the pasta and parsley and spoon it into a baking dish.
- Scatter over the mozzarella cubes then bake for 10 minutes or until the top is bubbling.

PREPARATION TIME 2 MINUTES

COOKING TIME 25 MINUTES

**INGREDIENTS**

400 g / 14 oz / 4 cups maccheroncini pasta
4 tbsp olive oil
200 g / 7 oz / 1 ¼ cups pancetta, cut into lardons
300 ml / 10 ½ fl. oz / 1 ¼ cups white wine
2 tbsp flat leaf parsley, finely chopped
150 g / 5 ½ oz / 1 ½ cups mozzarella, cubed

### Baked Maccheroncini with Chorizo and Mozzarella

 **402**

- Replace the pancetta with cubed chorizo.

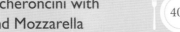

# Tagliatelle with Spring Vegetables

**403**

**SERVES 2**

PREPARATION TIME 2 MINUTES

COOKING TIME 12 MINUTES

### INGREDIENTS

200 g / 7 oz / 2 cups tagliatelle
1 carrot, sliced
6 asparagus spears, trimmed
75 g / 2 ½ oz / ¾ cup mange tout
75 g / 2 ½ oz / ½ cup fresh peas
4 tbsp olive oil
3 cloves garlic, crushed
75 g / 2 ½ oz / ½ cup fresh goats'
cheese
shredded fresh basil to garnish

- Cook the tagliatelle in boiling salted water according to the packet instructions or until al dente.
- Meanwhile, blanch the vegetables in boiling salted water for 3–4 minutes or until just tender. Drain well.
- Heat the oil in a sauté pan and fry the garlic for 2 minutes. Add the drained vegetables and cook, stirring occasionally, for 3 minutes so that they take on the flavour from the oil. Season to taste with salt and pepper.
- Reserve a couple of ladles of pasta water and drain the rest.
- Stir the pasta into the sauté pan with 3 tablespoons of the pasta water and shake to emulsify with the oil. If it looks a bit dry, add some more pasta water.
- Divide between 2 warm bowls, crumble over the goats' cheese and scatter with basil.

## Tagliatelle and Lemon

**404**

- Replace the vegetables with a sauce made from 200 ml / 7 fl. oz / ¾ cup double (heavy) cream and the zest and juice of a lemon, heated together in a small pan.

# Lemon and Asparagus Risotto

**405**

**SERVES 2**

PREPARATION TIME 5 MINUTES

COOKING TIME 30 MINUTES

### INGREDIENTS

1 l / 1 pt 15 fl. oz / 4 cups good
quality vegetable stock
2 tbsp olive oil
1 onion, finely chopped
2 cloves of garlic, crushed
1 lemon, zest finely pared
150 g / 5 ½ oz / ¾ cup risotto rice
100 g / 3 ½ oz / 1 cup asparagus
spears, cut into short lengths
2 tbsp butter
salt and pepper

- Heat the stock in a saucepan.
- Heat the olive oil in a sauté pan and gently fry the onion for 5 minutes without colouring.
- Add the garlic and lemon zest and cook for 2 more minutes then stir in the rice.
- When it is well coated with the oil, add the asparagus, followed by 2 ladles of the hot stock.
- Cook, stirring occasionally, until most of the stock has been absorbed before adding the next 2 ladles.
- Continue in this way for around 15 minutes or until the rice is just tender.
- Stir in the butter, then cover the pan and take off the heat to rest for 4 minutes.
- Uncover the pan and season well with salt and pepper, then spoon into warm bowls.

## Lemon and Pea Risotto

 **406**

- Replace the asparagus with 100 g / 3 ½ oz / 1 cup of mange tout and 75 g / 3 oz / ½ cup of defrosted frozen peas.

**407**

**SERVES 2**

# Tomato, Mushroom and Pepper Risotto

- Heat the stock and chopped tomatoes together in a saucepan.
- Heat the olive oil in a sauté pan and gently fry the onion and peppers for 5 minutes without colouring.
- Add the garlic and cook for 2 more minutes then stir in the mushrooms and rice.
- When they are well coated with the oil, add 2 ladles of the hot stock.
- Cook, stirring occasionally, until most of the stock has been absorbed before adding the next 2 ladles.
- Continue in this way for around 15 minutes or until the rice is just tender.
- Stir in the butter, then cover the pan and take off the heat to rest for 4 minutes.
- Uncover the pan and season well with salt and pepper, then spoon into warm bowls.
- Garnish with basil and serve.

### Tomato, Mushroom and Sausage Risotto

**408**

- Replace the pepper with 4 skinned pork sausages, broken into chunks.

PREPARATION TIME 5 MINUTES

COOKING TIME 30 MINUTES

### INGREDIENTS

500 ml / 17 ½ fl. oz / 2 cups vegetable stock
500 ml / 17 ½ fl. oz / 2 ¼ cups canned tomatoes, chopped
2 tbsp olive oil
1 onion, finely chopped
1 yellow pepper, deseeded and sliced
2 cloves of garlic, crushed
100 g / 3 ½ oz / 1 cup mushrooms, sliced
150 g / 5 ½ oz / ¾ cup risotto rice
2 tbsp butter
salt and pepper
basil leaves to garnish

**409**

**SERVES 2**

# Pesto Risotto

- Heat the stock in a saucepan.
- Heat the olive oil in a sauté pan and gently fry the onion for 5 minutes without colouring.
- Add the garlic and cook for 2 more minutes then stir in the rice.
- When it is well coated with the oil, add 2 ladles of the hot stock.
- Cook, stirring occasionally, until most of the stock has been absorbed before adding the next 2 ladles.
- Continue in this way for around 15 minutes or until the rice is just tender.
- Stir in the pesto and Parmesan, then cover the pan and take off the heat to rest for 4 minutes.
- Uncover the pan and season well with salt and pepper, then spoon into warm bowls.
- Garnish with rocket leaves and serve immediately.

### Pesto and Artichoke Risotto

**410**

- Add 200 g / 7 oz / 1 ⅓ cups of preserved baby artichokes in oil, 4 minutes before the end of the cooking time.

PREPARATION TIME 5 MINUTES

COOKING TIME 30 MINUTES

### INGREDIENTS

1 l / 1 pt 15 fl. oz / 4 cups good quality vegetable stock
2 tbsp olive oil
1 onion, finely chopped
2 cloves of garlic, crushed
150 g / 5 ½ oz / ¾ cup risotto rice
100 g / 3 ½ oz / ½ cup pesto
50 g / 1 ¾ oz / ½ cup Parmesan, finely grated
salt and pepper
a handful of rocket (arugula) leaves

# Savoury Pork and Apple Crumble

PREPARATION TIME 10 MINUTES

COOKING TIME 45 MINUTES

......................................................

## INGREDIENTS

2 tbsp butter
1 onion, sliced
450 g / 1 lb / 3 cups pork shoulder, cubed
salt and pepper
2 apples, chopped
250 ml / 9 fl. oz / 1 cup cider

### FOR THE CRUMBLE MIXTURE
75 g / 2 ½ oz / ⅓ cup butter
50 g / 1 ¾ oz / ⅓ cup plain (all purpose) flour
25 g / 1 oz ground almonds

- Preheat the oven to 180°C (160°C fan) / 355F / gas 4.
- Heat the butter in a sauté pan and fry the onion and pork with plenty of salt and pepper for 5 minutes or until starting to brown.
- Add the apples and cider and bring to a simmer then pour the mixture into a baking dish.
- Meanwhile, rub the butter into the flour and stir in the ground almonds, then season with salt and pepper.
- Take a handful of the topping and squeeze it into a clump, then crumble it over the pork.
- Repeat with the rest of the crumble mixture then press down with your fingertips into an even layer. Bake the crumble for 35 minutes or until the topping is golden brown.

# Beef Tartare and Sun-dried Tomato Bites

PREPARATION TIME 20 MINUTES

......................................................

## INGREDIENTS

350 g / 12 oz / 2 cups beef fillet
1 shallot, finely chopped
100 g / 3 ½ oz / ½ cup sun-dried tomatoes in oil, drained and chopped
1 tbsp grain mustard
2 tbsp tarragon, finely chopped
salt and pepper

### TO SERVE
12 little gem lettuce leaves
6 cherry tomatoes, halved

- Cut the beef into very thin slices with a sharp knife, then cut each slice into a fine julienne.
- Cut across the julienne strips into tiny squares then mix with the rest of the ingredients.
- Season the tartare to taste with salt and black pepper then roll the mixture into bite-sized balls.
- Serve each tartare bite inside a little gem leaf, garnished with tomato.

## 413

**SERVES 2**

# Baked Chicken with Camembert

- Preheat the oven to 200°C (180°C fan) / 390F / gas 6.
- Thinly slice the green ends of the onions then set aside and reserve. Cut the base of the onions in half and mix with the carrots and oil in a baking dish.
- Lay the chicken breasts on top, skin side up, and season well with salt and pepper.
- Bake for 30 minutes then lay the Camembert on top of the chicken and cook for another 5 minutes or until the chicken is cooked through.
- Divide between 2 warm bowls and sprinkle with the reserved onion tops.

PREPARATION TIME 10 MINUTES

COOKING TIME 35 MINUTES

### INGREDIENTS

8 salad onions
8 baby carrots, peeled and halved lengthways
2 tbsp olive oil
2 chicken breasts, skin on
salt and pepper
2 slices Camembert

---

## 414

**SERVES 6**

# Pot-roasted Marsala Chicken

PREPARATION TIME 10 MINUTES

COOKING TIME 40 MINUTES

### INGREDIENTS

700 ml / 1 pint 5 oz / 3 ½ cups chicken stock
300 ml / 10 ½ fl. oz / 1 ½ cups marsala

2 tbsp plain (all purpose) flour
1 tsp mustard powder
salt and pepper
1 chicken, jointed
2 tbsp olive oil
2 tbsp butter
100 g / 3 ½ oz / ½ cup sultanas
2 tbsp thyme leaves
2 tbsp flaked (slivered) almonds

- Preheat the oven to 200°C (180°C fan) / 390F / gas 6.
- Put the stock and marsala in a saucepan and bring to the boil as you prepare the chicken.
- Mix the flour with the mustard powder and a pinch of salt and pepper and dust it over the chicken pieces.
- Heat the oil and butter in a large cast iron casserole pan then brown the chicken pieces all over in 2 batches.
- Arrange them all in the pot and add the sultanas and thyme, then pour over the hot marsala and chicken stock.
- Transfer the dish to the oven and cook uncovered for 35–40 minutes.
- Pierce the thickest part of one of the chicken pieces. If the juices run clear, the meat is ready.
- Sprinkle over the almonds and serve.

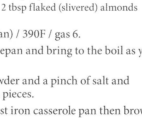

---

## 415

**SERVES 2**

# Marinated Squid Salad

PREPARATION TIME 40 MINUTES

### INGREDIENTS

8 baby squid tubes
1 lemon, juiced
2 tbsp balsamic vinegar
1 tsp sesame seeds
1 tsp black sesame seeds

1 red chilli (chili), finely chopped
2 tbsp basil leaves, shredded
1 jar roasted red peppers in oil, drained
3 tbsp olive oil
salt and pepper
a handful rocket (arugula) leaves
a handful baby spinach leaves

- Score a diamond pattern all over the squid then put the in a shallow bowl.
- Mix together the lemon juice, vinegar, sesame seeds, chilli and basil then pour it over the squid.
- Leave to stand for 30 minutes for the acid in the marinade to cure and 'cook' the squid.
- Stir the peppers and oil into the squid mixture and season with salt and pepper.
- Toss the salad with the leaves and serve immediately.

# Stir-fried Tofu with Vegetables

## Tofu in Black Bean Sauce

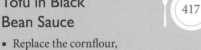
417

- Replace the cornflour, sherry and sugar with ½ jar of black bean sauce.

## Tofu in Oyster Sauce

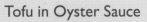

418

- Replace the cornflour, sherry and sugar with 4 tbsp of oyster sauce.

PREPARATION TIME 5 MINUTES

COOKING TIME 8 MINUTES

### INGREDIENTS

2 tbsp vegetable oil
2 cloves garlic, finely chopped
1 tbsp root ginger, finely chopped
200 g / 7 oz / 1 ¼ cups firm tofu, cubed
75 g / 2 ½ oz / ¾ cup baby sweetcorn, halved lengthways
75 g / 2 ½ oz / ¾ cup mange tout
½ tsp cornflour (cornstarch)
2 tbsp rice wine (mirin) or dry sherry
1 tsp caster (superfine) sugar
1 tbsp light soy sauce
75 g / 2 ½ oz / 1 ½ cups alfalfa sprouts
boiled rice to serve

- Heat the oil in a large wok and fry the garlic and ginger for 30 seconds.
- Add the tofu and stir-fry for 2 minutes then add the baby corn and mange tout and stir-fry for another 2 minutes.
- Mix the cornflour with the rice wine, sugar and soy and add it to the wok.
- Stir-fry for 2 more minutes then serve immediately, garnished with the alfalfa sprouts on a bed of rice.

419

SERVES 4

# Macaroni Cheese with Bacon

- Preheat the oven to 180°C (160°C fan) / 355F / gas 4.
- Cook the macaroni in boiling, salted water according to the packet instructions or until al dente. Drain well.
- Meanwhile, melt the butter in a medium saucepan then fry the bacon and courgettes for 2 minutes.
- Remove the bacon and courgettes from the pan with a slotted spoon, then stir the flour into the pan.
- Gradually whisk in the milk a little at a time until it is all incorporated. Cook the sauce over a low heat, stirring constantly, until the mixture thickens.
- Take the pan off the heat and stir in the bacon and courgettes and half the cheese. Season to taste.
- Stir the macaroni into the cheese sauce and scrape it into a baking dish.
- Sprinkle over the remaining cheese then bake for 25 minutes or until the cheese is bubbling.

PREPARATION TIME 5 MINUTES

COOKING TIME 40 MINUTES

### INGREDIENTS

400 g / 14 oz / 4 cups dried macaroni
25 g / 1 oz butter
4 rashers streaky bacon, chopped
2 courgettes (zucchinis), sliced
25 g / 1 oz / ¼ cup plain (all purpose) flour
600 ml / 1 pt / 2 ½ cups milk
150 g / 5 ½ oz / 1 ½ cups Cheddar cheese, grated
salt and pepper

## Chorizo Macaroni Cheese

420

- Omit the courgettes (zucchinis) and replace the bacon with small cubes of chorizo.

421

SERVES 4

# Tuna and Courgette Tortilla

- Heat half the oil in a non-stick frying pan and fry the courgettes for 5 minutes.
- Meanwhile, gently beat the eggs in a jug to break up the yolks. When the courgettes are ready, stir them into the eggs with the tuna and season with salt and pepper.
- Heat the rest of the oil in the frying pan then pour in the egg mixture.
- Cook over a gentle heat for 6–8 minutes or until the egg has set round the outside, but the centre is still a bit runny.
- Turn it out onto a plate, then slide it back into the pan and cook the other side for 4–6 minutes.
- Leave to cool for 5 minutes then cut into wedges and serve, garnished with oregano.

PREPARATION TIME 10 MINUTES

COOKING TIME 20 MINUTES

### INGREDIENTS

4 tbsp olive oil
1 courgette (zucchini), quartered and sliced
6 eggs
200 g / 7 oz / 1 cup canned tuna, drained and flaked
salt and pepper
oregano to garnish

## Courgette and Dill Tortilla

422

- Omit the tuna and stir 2 tbsp of chopped dill into the egg mixture.

# Chicken Enchiladas

**PREPARATION TIME 10 MINUTES**

**COOKING TIME 20 MINUTES**

......................................................

## INGREDIENTS

2 tbsp vegetable oil
2 chicken breasts, diced
200 g / 7 oz / 2 cups button mushrooms, quartered
2 tbsp soured cream
150 g / 5 ½ oz / 1 ½ cups mild cheese, grated
4 corn tortillas
50 g / 1 ¾ oz / ⅓ cup Jalapenos, sliced

- Preheat the oven to 200°C (180°C fan) / 390F / gas 6.
- Heat the oil in a frying pan and fry the chicken and mushrooms for 5 minutes or until cooked through.
- Stir in the soured cream and half of the cheese, then divide the mixture between the 4 tortillas.
- Fold them round and arrange in a snugly fitting baking dish.
- Sprinkle over the rest of the cheese and arrange the jalapenos in a line on top then bake for 10–15 minutes or until the cheese has melted and the edges are toasted.

### Chilli Enchiladas  424

- Replace the chicken filling with chilli con carne.

---

 425

**SERVES 4**

# Sticky Sesame Chicken

**PREPARATION TIME 5 MINUTES**

**COOKING TIME 35–40 MINUTES**

......................................................

## INGREDIENTS

8 chicken thighs
2 tbsp runny honey
2 tbsp soy sauce
½ orange, juiced
2 tbsp oyster sauce
½ tsp Chinese five spice powder
2 tsp sesame oil
2 tbsp sesame seeds
rice noodles and chives to serve

- Preheat the oven to 200°C (180°C fan) / 390F / gas 6.
- Arrange the chicken thighs in a single layer in a snugly-fitting baking dish.
- Mix the honey, soy, orange juice, oyster sauce, five spice and sesame oil together and pour it over the chicken.
- Sprinkle with sesame seeds and bake for 35–40 minutes or until the chicken is cooked through.
- If it starts to colour too quickly, cover the dish with foil.
- Serve the chicken with rice noodles, garnished with chives.

### Sticky Sesame Pork 426

- Replace the chicken thighs with pork spare rib chops.

427

SERVES 1

# White Asparagus Omelette

### Preserved Artichoke Omelette

428

- Replace the asparagus with a jar of preserved baby artichokes.

### Antipasti Omelette

429

- Replace the asparagus with a jar of mixed antipasti in oil.

PREPARATION TIME 2 MINUTES

COOKING TIME 4 MINUTES

## INGREDIENTS

3 large eggs
salt and pepper
1 tbsp butter
1 tbsp flat leaf parsley, finely chopped
75 g / 2 ½ oz / ¾ cup canned white asparagus, drained

- Break the eggs into a jug with a pinch of salt and pepper and beat them gently to break up the yolks.
- Heat the butter in a non-stick frying pan until sizzling then pour in the eggs.
- Cook over a medium heat until the eggs start to set around the outside. Use a spatula to draw the sides of the omelette into the centre and tilt the pan to fill the gaps with more liquid egg.
- Sprinkle with parsley and arrange the asparagus on top then continue cooking until the top of the omelette is just set.
- Shake the omelette out onto a plate, folding it over as you go.

**SERVES 6–8**

# Leek, Tomato and Cheese Quiche

## Quiche Lorraine

431

- Replace the tomatoes with smoked bacon lardons.

## Tomato and Chorizo Quiche

432

- Replace the leeks with a chopped onion and add 150 g / 5 oz / ¾ cup cubed chorizo with the tomatoes.

PREPARATION TIME 5 MINUTES

COOKING TIME 40 MINUTES

### INGREDIENTS

2 leeks, sliced
2 tbsp butter
3 large eggs, beaten
225 ml / 8 fl. oz / 1 cup double (heavy) cream
100 g / 3 ½ oz / ¾ cup cherry tomatoes, quartered
150 g / 5 ½ oz / 1 ½ cups Gruyère, grated
salt and pepper
1 ready-made pastry case

- Preheat the oven to 150ºC (130ºC fan) / 300F / gas 2.
- Fry the leeks in the butter with a pinch of salt for 5 minutes or until starting to soften.
- Whisk the eggs with the double cream until smoothly combined then stir in the leeks, tomatoes and half of the Gruyère. Season generously with salt and pepper.
- Pour the filling into the pastry case and scatter the rest of the cheese on top.
- Bake for 35 minutes or until just set in the centre.

**433**

**SERVES 2**

# Smoked Chicken Risotto

- Heat the stock in a saucepan.
- Heat the olive oil in a sauté pan and gently fry the onion for 5 minutes without colouring.
- Add the garlic and cook for 2 more minutes then stir in the rice.
- When it is well coated with the oil, add 2 ladles of the hot stock.
- Cook, stirring occasionally, until most of the stock has been absorbed before adding the next 2 ladles.
- Continue in this way for around 15 minutes or until the rice is just tender.
- Stir in the Parmesan and season with salt and pepper. Cover the pan and take off the heat to rest for 4 minutes.
- Spoon the risotto into warm bowls and lay the smoked chicken slices on top.

PREPARATION TIME 5 MINUTES

COOKING TIME 30 MINUTES

### INGREDIENTS

1 l / 1 pt 15 fl. oz / 4 cups good
quality chicken stock
2 tbsp olive oil
1 onion, finely chopped
2 cloves of garlic, crushed
150 g / 5 ½ oz / ¾ cup risotto rice
50 g / 1 ¾ oz / ½ cup Parmesan,
finely grated
salt and pepper
1 smoked chicken breast, sliced

### Smoked Chicken
### and Broad Bean Risotto

**434**

- Add 200 g / 7 oz / 1 ⅓ cups of fresh baby broad beans to the risotto, 8 minutes before the end.

**435**

**SERVES 6–8**

# Curried Leek and Potato Quiche

- Preheat the oven to 150°C (130°C fan) / 300F / gas 2
- Fry the leeks in the butter with a pinch of salt for 5 minutes or until starting to soften then stir in the curry powder and potatoes. Warm through for 2 minutes.
- Whisk the eggs with the double cream until smoothly combined then stir in the leeks, potatoes and half of the Emmental. Season generously with salt and pepper.
- Pour the filling into the pastry case and scatter the rest of the cheese on top.
- Bake for 35 minutes or until just set in the centre.

PREPARATION TIME 5 MINUTES

COOKING TIME 45 MINUTES

### INGREDIENTS

2 leeks, sliced
2 tbsp butter
2 tsp mild curry powder
4 boiled potatoes, cooled and cubed
3 large eggs, beaten
225 ml / 8 fl. oz / 1 cup double
(heavy) cream
150 g / 5 ½ oz / 1 ½ cups Emmental,
grated
salt and pepper
1 ready-made pastry case

### Curried Leek and
### Chicken Quiche

 **436**

- Replace the potatoes with 150 g / 5 oz / ¾ cup of cooked, cubed chicken breast.

SERVES 4

# Leek and Mince Hot Pot

PREPARATION TIME 10 MINUTES

COOKING TIME 40 MINUTES

......................................................

### INGREDIENTS

400 g / 14 oz / 2 ¼ cups maris piper
potatoes, peeled and sliced
4 tbsp butter
2 leeks, sliced
200 g / 7 oz / 1 cup minced lamb
200 ml / 7 fl. oz / 1 cup white wine
1 tbsp flat leaf parsley, finely
chopped
75 g / 2 ½ oz / ½ cup Red Leicester,
grated

- Preheat the oven to 220°C (200°C fan) / 430F / gas 7
  and put a baking dish in to heat.
- Cook the potatoes in boiling salted water for 10
  minutes or until tender. Drain well.
- Meanwhile, heat the butter in a frying pan and cook the
  leeks with a pinch of salt for 5 minutes.
- Add the mince and stir-fry for 3 minutes then stir in
  the wine and bring to a simmer.
- Spoon the mince into the preheated baking dish and
  arrange the potatoes on top.
- Sprinkle over the parsley, followed by the cheese, then
  bake for 30 minutes or until the potatoes are golden.

## Mince and Pea Hot Pot

438

- Replace the leeks with 200 g / 7 oz / 1 ½
  cups of defrosted frozen peas.

SERVES 8

# Savoury Leek and Stilton Crumble

PREPARATION TIME 5 MINUTES

COOKING TIME 45 MINUTES

......................................................

### INGREDIENTS

2 tbsp butter
3 leeks, chopped
salt and pepper
4 boiled potatoes, cooled and cubed
150 g / 5 ½ oz / 1 cup Stilton, cubed

### FOR THE CRUMBLE MIXTURE

75 g / 2 ½ oz / ⅓ cup butter
50 g / 1 ¾ oz / ⅓ cup plain (all
purpose) flour
25 g / 1 oz / ¼ cup ground almonds

- Preheat the oven to 180°C (160°C fan) / 355F / gas 4.
- Heat the butter in a sauté pan and fry the leeks with
  plenty of salt and pepper for 5 minutes or until
  starting to soften.
- Mix in the potatoes and Stilton then spoon the mixture
  into a baking dish.
- While the leeks are cooking, rub the butter into the
  flour and stir in the ground almonds, then season
  with salt and pepper.
- Take a handful of the topping and squeeze it into a
  clump, then crumble it over the leeks.
- Repeat with the rest of the crumble mixture then
  press down with your fingertips into an even layer.
  Bake the crumble for 35 minutes or until the topping
  is golden brown.

## Parsnip and Stilton Crumble

440

- Replace the boiled potatoes with
  boiled parsnips.

441

SERVES 4

# Thai Red Chicken Curry

## Thai Red Aubergine Curry

442

- Replace the chicken with a cubed aubergine (eggplant).

## Thai Red Salmon Curry

443

- Replace the chicken with an equal weight of cubed salmon fillet, but add it right at the end and heat through for 2 minutes or until just opaque inside.

PREPARATION TIME 5 MINUTES

COOKING TIME 10 MINUTES

### INGREDIENTS

2 tbsp vegetable oil
2 tbsp Thai red curry paste
2 fresh or frozen kaffir lime leaves
2 skinless chicken breasts, cut into chunks
400 ml / 14 fl. oz / 2 cups coconut milk
1 tsp caster (superfine) sugar
1 tbsp fish sauce
2 tbsp coriander (cilantro) leaves, chopped
jasmine rice to serve

- Heat the oil in a wok and fry the curry paste and lime leaves for 2 minutes.
- Add the chicken to the wok and stir-fry for 4 minutes then add the coconut milk and bring to a simmer.
- Season to taste with the caster sugar and fish sauce before serving in warm bowls, garnished with coriander.
- Serve with jasmine rice.

## 444

**SERVES 4**

# Smoked Haddock and Leek Pie

**PREPARATION TIME 10 MINUTES**

**COOKING TIME 35 MINUTES**

### INGREDIENTS

450 g / 1 lb / 2 ½ cups maris piper potatoes, peeled and cubed
600 ml / 1 pint / 2 ½ cups whole milk
450 g / 1 lb / 2 ¼ cups smoked haddock
3 tbsp butter
1 leek, chopped
1 tbsp plain (all purpose) flour
1 tsp Dijon mustard
75 g / 2 ½ oz / ¾ cup Emmental, grated

- Cook the potatoes in boiling salted water for 15 minutes or until tender. Drain well.
- Meanwhile, bring the milk to a simmer then pour it over the smoked haddock. Cover the dish with clingfilm and leave to steep for 10 minutes.
- Drain off and reserve the milk and flake the haddock, discarding any skin and bones.
- When the potatoes are ready, mash them until smooth with 1 tablespoon of the butter and a little of the haddock milk.
- Heat the rest of the butter in a saucepan and fry the leeks for 5 minutes.
- Stir in the flour then gradually incorporate the rest of the haddock milk, stirring continuously to avoid any lumps forming.
- Continue to stir until it starts to bubble then stir in the mustard and flaked haddock.
- Preheat the grill to its highest setting.
- Pour the haddock mixture into a baking dish and top with the mashed potato.
- Sprinkle over the Emmental and grill for 5 minutes or until the top is golden and bubbling.

## 445

**SERVES 4**

# Tartiflette

**PREPARATION TIME 5 MINUTES**

**COOKING TIME 40 MINUTES**

### INGREDIENTS

800 g / 1 lb 12 oz / 4 ½ cups maris piper potatoes, peeled and cubed
2 tbsp olive oil
1 onion, thinly sliced
150 g / 5 ½ oz / 1 cup smoked lardons
4 tbsp crème fraîche
200 g / 7 oz / 2 cups Reblochon, sliced

- Boil the potatoes in salted water for 12 minutes or until tender then drain well.
- Meanwhile, heat the oil in a sauté pan and fry the onion and lardons for 5 minutes.
- Stir in the crème fraîche and drained potatoes, then spoon the mixture into a baking dish.
- Lay the cheese on top and bake for 25 minutes or until golden brown.

## 446 — SERVES 4 — Penne with Smoked Trout

- Preheat the oven to 220°C (200°C fan) / 430F / gas 7.
- Cook the penne in boiling salted water according to the packet instructions or until al dente. Drain well.
- Mix the crème fraîche with the trout and watercress then stir in the pasta and season with salt and pepper.
- Spoon it into a baking dish and sprinkle with Emmental then bake for 15 minutes or until the top is golden.

PREPARATION TIME 5 MINUTES

COOKING TIME 30 MINUTES

### INGREDIENTS

400 g / 14 oz / 4 cups penne
300 ml / 10 ½ oz / 1 ¼ cups crème fraîche
150 g / 5 ½ oz / 1 cup smoked trout, chopped
50 g / 1 ¾ oz / 2 cups watercress
salt and pepper
50 g / 1 ¾ oz / ½ cup Emmental, grated

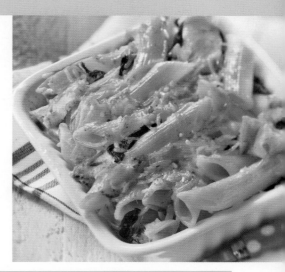

## Cheese and Leek Crustless Quiche — 447 — SERVES 4

PREPARATION TIME 5 MINUTES

COOKING TIME 30–35 MINUTES

### INGREDIENTS

3 leeks, chopped
2 tbsp butter
salt and pepper

5 free-range eggs
2 tbsp crème fraîche
75 g / 2 ½ oz / ¾ cup Gruyere, grated

- Preheat the oven to 180°C (160°C fan) / 355F / gas 4.
- Fry the leeks in the butter with plenty of salt and pepper for 10 minutes or until softened.
- Lightly beat the eggs with the crème fraîche then stir in the leeks.
- Pour the mixture into a baking dish and sprinkle over the cheese then bake in the oven for 20–25 minutes or until just set in the centre.
- Serve warm or at room temperature.

## Red Pepper and Asparagus Paella — 448 — SERVES 4

PREPARATION TIME 5 MINUTES

COOKING TIME 30 MINUTES

### INGREDIENTS

1 l / 1 pt 15 fl. oz / 4 cups good quality vegetable stock
4 tbsp olive oil
1 onion, finely chopped

2 cloves of garlic, crushed
100 g / 3 ½ oz / 1 cup asparagus spears, cut into short lengths
1 courgette (zucchini), sliced
200 g / 7 oz / 1 cup paella rice
salt and pepper
1 red pepper, deseeded and sliced
2 tbsp flat leaf parsley, chopped

- Heat the stock in a saucepan.
- Heat the olive oil in a paella pan and gently fry the onion for 5 minutes without colouring.
- Add the garlic and cook for 2 more minutes then stir in the vegetables and rice and season with salt and pepper.
- Stir well to coat with the oil, then pour in the stock and stir once more.
- Arrange the pepper slices on top and bring to a simmer, then cook without stirring for 10 minutes.
- Cover the pan with foil or a lid, turn off the heat and leave to stand for 10 minutes.
- Uncover the pan and sprinkle over the parsley before serving.

# DESSERTS

449

SERVES 4

# Pear Kebabs with Toffee Sauce

PREPARATION TIME 25 MINUTES

COOKING TIME 6 MINUTES

......................................................

## INGREDIENTS

4 pears, cored and cubed
2 tbsp butter, melted

### FOR THE TOFFEE SAUCE

100 g / 3 ½ oz / ½ cup butter
100 g / 3 ½ oz / ½ cup muscovado sugar
100 g / 3 ½ oz / ½ cup golden syrup
100 ml / 3 ½ fl. oz / ½ cup double (heavy) cream

- Soak 12 wooden skewers in cold water for 20 minutes then preheat the grill to its highest setting.
- Thread the pears onto the skewers and brush with melted butter.
- Grill the kebabs for 3 minutes on each side or until the pears are golden brown.
- Meanwhile, put the toffee sauce ingredients in a small saucepan and stir over a low heat until the butter melts and the sugar dissolves.
- Bring the toffee sauce to the boil then take it off the heat.
- Divide the kebabs between 4 warm plates and drizzle with toffee sauce.

### Toffee Apple Kebabs  450

- Replace the pears with apples.

451

SERVES 4

# Strawberry and Kumquat Salad

PREPARATION TIME 5 MINUTES

......................................................

## INGREDIENTS

200 g / 7 oz / 1 cup strawberries, halved
100 g / 3 ½ oz / ¾ cup kumquats, sliced
1 tsp coriander (cilantro) seeds, crushed
1 tsp runny honey
1 tbsp lemon juice
2 tbsp extra virgin olive oil
4 sprigs mint

- Mix the strawberries with the kumquats and divide between 4 bowls.
- Put the coriander seeds, honey, lemon juice and oil in a jar and shake together to emulsify.
- Pour the dressing over the salad and garnish with a sprig of mint.

### Plum and Kumquat Salad  452

- Replace the strawberries with 6 plums that have been stoned and cut into eighths.

**SERVES 4** # Spiced Pear and Pineapple Kebabs

- Soak 8 wooden skewers in cold water for 20 minutes.
- Meanwhile, put the honey in a small saucepan with the spices and heat gently. Leave to infuse for 15 minutes.
- Preheat the grill to its highest setting.
- Thread alternate chunks of pear and pineapple onto the skewers and brush with the spiced honey.
- Grill the kebabs for 3 minutes on each side or until the edges of the fruit start to caramelise.
- Transfer the kebabs to 4 warm plates and garnish with star anise and mint sprigs.

PREPARATION TIME 30 MINUTES

COOKING TIME 10 MINUTES

### INGREDIENTS

4 tbsp runny honey
1 star anise, plus extra to garnish
4 cloves
2 pears, quartered, cored and sliced
½ pineapple, peeled, cored and cut into large chunks
a few sprigs of mint

## Spiced Pineapple and Mango Kebabs  454

- Replace the pear with chunks of fresh mango.

**SERVES 4** # Mango, Banana and Lime Crumble

- Preheat the oven to 180°C (160°C fan) / 355F / gas 4.
- Mix the fruit with the lime juice and zest and tip it into a baking dish.
- Rub the butter into the flour and stir in the ground almonds and brown sugar.
- Take a handful of the topping and squeeze it into a clump, then crumble it over the fruit.
- Repeat with the rest of the crumble mixture then bake for 40 minutes or until the topping is golden brown.

PREPARATION TIME 12 MINUTES

COOKING TIME 40 MINUTES

### INGREDIENTS

1 mango, peeled, stoned and cubed
2 bananas, peeled and cut into chunks
1 lime, juiced and zest finely grated
75 g / 2 ½ oz / ⅓ cup butter
50 g / 1 ¾ oz / ⅓ cup plain (all purpose) flour
25 g / 1 oz / ¼ cup ground almonds
40 g / 1 ½ oz / ¼ cup light brown sugar

## Tropical Coconut Crumble  456

- Replace the ground almonds in the crumble topping with desiccated coconut.

# Peaches with Mascarpone and Honey

457

SERVES 4

PREPARATION TIME 10 MINUTES

COOKING TIME 10 MINUTES

### INGREDIENTS

6 peaches, halved and stoned
250 g / 9 oz / 1 cup mascarpone
50 g / 1 ¾ oz / ½ cup flaked (slivered) almonds
4 tbsp runny honey
black pepper

- Preheat the oven to 180°C (160°C fan) / 355F / gas 4.
- Arrange the peaches in a large baking dish and top each one with a spoonful of mascarpone.
- Sprinkle the peaches with flaked (slivered) almonds and drizzle with honey then grind over a little black pepper.
- Bake the peaches for 10 minutes or until the flesh is soft and the almonds are toasted.

### Baked Apricots with Pistachios  458

- Replace the peaches with apricots and substitute the almonds with pistachio nuts.

# Marinated Strawberries and Kumquats

459

SERVES 4

PREPARATION TIME 35 MINUTES

COOKING TIME 5 MINUTES

### INGREDIENTS

200 g / 7 oz / 1 cup strawberries, halved
100 g / 3 ½ oz / ¾ cup kumquats, halved
3 tbsp runny honey
1 tbsp Cointreau
4 dried lemon verbena leaves
1 tbsp granulated sugar

- Mix the strawberries with the kumquats in a shallow bowl.
- Put the honey, Cointreau and lemon verbena in a small saucepan with 3 tablespoons of water and bring to a simmer.
- Pour the marinade over the fruit and leave to macerate for 35 minutes.
- Sprinkle with granulated sugar just before serving.

### Marinated Pineapple and Kumquats  460

- Replace the strawberries with half a fresh pineapple, cut into cubes.

**461**

**SERVES 4**

# Raspberry Eton Mess

## Classic Eton Mess

**462**

- Replace the raspberries with sliced strawberries, but use a food processor rather than a sieve to make the sauce.

## Raspberry Fool

**463**

- Omit the meringue and replace half of the whipped cream with ready-made chilled custard.

**PREPARATION TIME 20 MINUTES**

### INGREDIENTS

300 g / 10 ½ oz / 2 ¼ cups raspberries
icing (confectioners') sugar to taste
600 ml / 1 pt / 2 ½ cups double (heavy) cream
4 meringue nests, crushed

- Press half the raspberries through a sieve to make a smooth sauce and discard the pips. Stir in icing sugar, a tbsp at a time, to achieve the right level of sweetness.
- Whip the cream until it forms soft peaks then fold in the meringue pieces and all but 4 of the whole raspberries.
- Swirl through the raspberry sauce and divide it between 4 sundae glasses then top each one with a raspberry.

**464**

**SERVES 4**

# Natillas

## Banana Custard

**465**

- Add a sliced banana to the bottom of each bowl and replace the cinnamon with a sprinkle of desiccated coconut.

## Blancmange Bowls

**466**

- Increase the quantity of cornflour to 4 tsp and chill the bowls in the fridge after filling.

PREPARATION TIME 10 MINUTES

COOKING TIME 15 MINUTES

### INGREDIENTS

450 ml / 12 ½ fl. oz / 1 ¾ cup whole milk
4 large egg yolks
75 g / 2 ½ oz / ⅓ cup caster (superfine) sugar
2 tsp cornflour (cornstarch)
1 tsp ground cinnamon

- Pour the milk into a saucepan and bring to simmering point.
- Meanwhile, whisk the egg yolks with the sugar and cornflour until thick.
- Gradually incorporate the hot milk, whisking all the time, then scrape the mixture back into the saucepan.
- Stir the custard over a low heat until it thickens then divide it between 4 bowls.
- Sprinkle the tops with cinnamon and leave for 10 minutes for a skin to form.

**467**

SERVES 4

# Griddled Pineapple with Vanilla and Honey

- Put the honey in a small saucepan with the vanilla and infuse over a low heat for 5 minutes.
- Pour the honey over the pineapple slices and leave to marinate for 20 minutes.
- Heat a griddle pan until smoking hot.
- Griddle the pineapple slices for 2 minutes on each side or until nicely marked, then divide between 4 warm plates and serve.

PREPARATION TIME 25 MINUTES

COOKING TIME 10 MINUTES

### INGREDIENTS

100 g / 3 ½ oz / ½ cup runny honey
1 vanilla pod, halved lengthways
1 pineapple, peeled, cored and sliced

### Griddled Pineapple with Chilli and Honey

 **468**

- Replace the vanilla pod with ½ tsp of dried chilli (chili) flakes.

**469**

SERVES 4

# Brioche and Apricot Pudding

- Preheat the oven to 180°C (160°C fan) / 355F / gas 4.
- Spread the brioche with butter and arrange the slices in a baking dish with the apricot pieces scattered throughout.
- Whisk the milk, cream, eggs and sugar together and pour it over the top, then press down on the brioche to help it soak up the liquid.
- Bake for 35–40 minutes or until the top is golden brown.

PREPARATION TIME 15 MINUTES

COOKING TIME 35–40 MINUTES

### INGREDIENTS

1 brioche loaf, sliced
3 tbsp butter, softened
75 g / 2 ½ oz / ⅓ cup dried apricots, chopped
250 ml / 9 fl. oz / 1 cup whole milk
200 ml / 7 oz / ¾ cup double (heavy) cream
4 large egg yolks
75 g / 2 ½ oz / ⅓ cup caster (superfine) sugar

### Apricot Croissant and Butter Pudding

 **470**

- Replace the brioche with 4 croissants that have been halved horizontally and omit the butter.

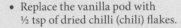

**SERVES 8**

# Apricot Upside-down Cake

PREPARATION TIME 10 MINUTES

COOKING TIME 35 MINUTES

## INGREDIENTS

300 g / 10 ½ oz / 2 cups self-raising flour
2 tsp baking powder
250 g / 9 oz / 1 ¼ cups caster (superfine) sugar
250 g / 9 oz / 1 ¼ cups butter, softened
5 large eggs
4 tbsp raspberry jam (jelly)
6 apricots, halved and stoned

- Preheat the oven to 170°C (150°C fan) / 340F / gas 3 and butter a 23 cm (9 in) round cake tin.
- Sieve the flour and baking powder into a mixing bowl and add the sugar, butter and eggs.
- Beat the mixture with an electric whisk for 4 minutes or until smooth and well whipped.
- Spread the jam over the base of the cake tin and arrange the apricots on top.
- Spoon in the cake mixture and bake for 35 minutes or until a skewer inserted in the centre comes out clean.
- Turn the cake out of the tin and serve warm or at room temperature.

### Peach Melba Upside-down Cake  472

- Replace the apricots with peaches.

**SERVES 4**

# Coconut Crème Brulee

PREPARATION TIME 35 MINUTES

COOKING TIME 10 MINUTES

## INGREDIENTS

450 ml / 12 ½ fl. oz / 1 ¾ cup whole milk
4 large egg yolks
75 g / 2 ½ oz / ⅓ cup caster (superfine) sugar
2 tsp cornflour (cornstarch)
4 tbsp desiccated coconut
4 tsp Demerara sugar

- Pour the milk into a saucepan and bring to simmering point.
- Meanwhile, whisk the egg yolks with the caster sugar, cornflour and coconut until thick.
- Gradually incorporate the hot milk, whisking all the time, then scrape the mixture back into the saucepan.
- Stir the custard over a low heat until it thickens then divide it between 4 ramekins.
- Chill in the fridge for 25 minutes.
- Sprinkle the tops with Demerara sugar then caramelise with a blow torch or under a hot grill.

### Coconut Banana Crème Brulee  474

- Divide 2 sliced bananas between the ramekin dishes before pouring the custard on top.

SERVES 8

# Lemon Tart

475

## Lime Tart

476
- Replace the lemons with 5 limes.

## Pink Grapefruit Tart

477
- Replace the lemons with a large grapefruit.

PREPARATION TIME 5 MINUTES

COOKING TIME 25–30 MINUTES

### INGREDIENTS

3 lemons, juiced
175 g / 6 oz / ¾ cup caster (superfine) sugar
2 tsp cornflour (cornstarch)
4 large eggs, beaten
225 ml / 8 fl.oz / ¾ cup double (heavy) cream
1 pastry case
lemon zest to garnish

- Preheat the oven to 170°C (150°C fan) / 340F / gas 3.
- Stir the lemon juice into the caster sugar and cornflour to dissolve, then whisk in the eggs and cream.
- Strain the mixture into the pastry case and bake for 25–30 minutes or until just set in the centre.
- Garnish with lemon zest and serve warm or at room temperature.

# 478

SERVES 4

# Apple Crumble Tatin

PREPARATION TIME 10 MINUTES

COOKING TIME 40 MINUTES

### INGREDIENTS

50 g / 1 ¾ oz / ¼ cup granulated sugar
450 g / 1 lb / 4 ¼ cups eating apples, peeled, cored and cut into wedges
75 g / 2 ½ oz / ⅓ cup butter
50 g / 1 ¾ oz / ⅓ cup plain (all purpose) flour
30 g / 1 oz / ½ cup ground almonds
30 g / 1 oz / ¼ cup blanched almonds, chopped
40 g / 1 ½ oz / ¼ cup light brown sugar

- Preheat the oven to 180°C (160°C fan) / 355F / gas 4.
- Put the granulated sugar in a saucepan and heat gently without stirring until it starts to turn to caramel round the edges.
- Continue to cook, swirling the pan occasionally, until it is all liquid, then pour the caramel into a buttered spring-form cake tin.
- Arrange the apples on top.
- Rub the butter into the flour and stir in the ground almonds, chopped almonds and brown sugar.
- Take a handful of the topping and squeeze it into a clump, then crumble it over the fruit.
- Repeat with the rest of the crumble mixture then bake for 30 minutes or until the topping is golden brown.
- Leave to cool for 5 minutes then carefully turn the crumble out onto a serving plate.

### Pear Crumble Tatin  479

- Replace the apples with pears.

# 480

SERVES 4

# Plum and Almond Crumble

PREPARATION TIME 12 MINUTES

COOKING TIME 40 MINUTES

### INGREDIENTS

450 g / 1 lb / 4 ½ cups plums, halved and stoned
2 tbsp caster (superfine) sugar
75 g / 2 ½ oz / ⅓ cup butter
50 g / 1 ¾ oz / ⅓ cup plain (all purpose) flour
30 g / 1 oz / ¼ cup ground almonds
30 g / 1 oz / ¼ cup flaked (slivered) almonds
40 g / 1 ½ oz / ¼ cup light brown sugar

- Preheat the oven to 180°C (160°C fan) / 355F / gas 4.
- Toss the plums with the caster sugar and arrange in a baking dish.
- Rub the butter into the flour and stir in the ground almonds, flaked almonds and brown sugar.
- Take a handful of the topping and squeeze it into a clump, then crumble it over the fruit.
- Repeat with the rest of the crumble mixture then bake for 40 minutes or until the topping is golden brown.

### Cherry and Marzipan Crumble  481

- Replace the plums with the same weight of stoned cherries and add 150 g / 5 oz / 1 cup of marzipan in small cubes to the crumble topping.

## 482
**SERVES 4**

# Apple and Raspberry Crumble

- Preheat the oven to 180°C (160°C fan) / 355F / gas 4.
- Mix the fruit with the caster sugar and tip it into a baking dish.
- Rub the butter into the flour and stir in the ground almonds and brown sugar.
- Take a handful of the topping and squeeze it into a clump, then crumble it over the fruit.
- Repeat with the rest of the crumble mixture then bake for 40 minutes or until the topping is golden brown.

**PREPARATION TIME 12 MINUTES**

**COOKING TIME 40 MINUTES**

### INGREDIENTS

1 Bramley apple, peeled and chopped
200 g / 7 oz / 1 ¾ cup raspberries
4 tbsp caster (superfine) sugar
75 g / 2 ½ oz / ⅓ cup butter
50 g / 1 ¾ oz / ⅓ cup plain (all purpose) flour
25 g / 1 oz / ¼ cup ground almonds
40 g / 1 ½ oz / ¼ cup light brown sugar

### Pear and Blueberry Crumble

### 483

- Replace the apples with pears and substitute blueberries for the raspberries.

## 484
**SERVES 4**

# Crêpes with Honey

- Sieve the flour into a bowl and make a well in the centre. Break in the egg and pour in the milk then use a whisk to gradually incorporate all of the flour from round the outside.
- Melt the butter in a small frying pan then whisk it into the batter.
- Put the buttered frying pan back over a low heat. Add a small ladle of batter and swirl the pan to coat the bottom.
- When it starts to dry and curl up at the edges, turn the pancake over with a spatula and cook the other side until golden brown and cooked through.
- Repeat with the rest of the mixture then serve the crêpes drizzled with honey.

**PREPARATION TIME 10 MINUTES**

**COOKING TIME 20 MINUTES**

### INGREDIENTS

150 g / 5 ½ oz / 1 cup plain (all purpose) flour
1 large egg
325 ml / 11 ½ fl. oz / 1 ⅓ cup whole milk
30 g / 1 oz butter, melted
6 tbsp runny honey

### Crêpes with Honey and Lemon

### 485

- Stir the zest and juice of a lemon into the honey before drizzling it over the crêpes.

**486**

SERVES 4

# Crêpes with Chocolate Dipping Sauce

PREPARATION TIME 10 MINUTES

COOKING TIME 20 MINUTES

## INGREDIENTS

150 g / 5 ½ oz / 1 cup plain (all purpose) flour
1 large egg
325 ml / 11 ½ fl. oz / 1 ⅓ cup whole milk
30 g / 1 oz butter, melted

### FOR THE DIPPING SAUCE

100 ml / 3 ½ fl. oz / ½ cup double (heavy) cream
1 tbsp brandy
100 g / 3 ½ oz / ¾ cup dark chocolate (minimum 60 % cocoa solids), chopped

- To make the dipping sauce, heat the cream and brandy to simmering point then pour it over the chocolate and stir to emulsify. Spoon into 4 serving glasses.
- Sieve the flour into a bowl and make a well in the centre. Break in the egg and pour in the milk then use a whisk to gradually incorporate all of the flour from round the outside.
- Melt the butter in a small frying pan then whisk it into the batter.
- Put the buttered frying pan back over a low heat. Add a small ladle of batter and swirl the pan to coat the bottom.
- When it starts to dry and curl up at the edges, turn the pancake over with a spatula and cook the other side until golden brown and cooked through.
- Repeat with the rest of the mixture then fold the crêpes into quarters and serve with the dipping sauce.

**487**

SERVES 4

# Cherry Fool

PREPARATION TIME 10 MINUTES

## INGREDIENTS

150 g / 5 ½ oz / ¾ cup cherries, stoned
2 tbsp kirsch
50 g / 1 ¾ oz / ½ cup icing (confectioners') sugar
600 ml / 1 pint / 2 ½ cups double (heavy) cream

- Put two-thirds of the cherries, the kirsch and icing sugar in a food processor and pulse until finely chopped.
- Whip the cream until thick then fold through the cherry mixture. Slice the remaining cherries and fold in.
- Spoon the mixture into 4 fool glasses and serve.

**488**

SERVES 4

# Milk Chocolate Crumble Pots

- Preheat the oven to 180°C (160°C fan) / 355F / gas 4.
- Heat the cream to simmering point then pour it over the chocolate and stir until smooth.
- Divide the mixture between 4 ramekins and chill for 35 minutes.
- Rub the butter into the flour and stir in the ground almonds, chopped almonds and brown sugar.
- Crumble the mixture onto a baking tray and bake for 25 minutes or until golden and crisp.
- Leave the crumble to cool for 5 minutes then sprinkle it over the chocolate pots.

PREPARATION TIME 45 MINUTES

COOKING TIME 30 MINUTES

### INGREDIENTS

200 ml / 7 fl. oz / ¾ cup double (heavy) cream
200 g / 7 oz / 1 ½ cups milk chocolate, chopped
**FOR THE CRUMBLE**
75 g / 2 ½ oz / ⅓ cup butter
50 g / 1 ¾ oz / ⅓ cup plain (all purpose) flour
30 g / 1 oz / ¼ cup ground almonds
30 g / 1 oz / ¼ cup blanched almonds, chopped
40 g / 1 ½ oz / ¼ cup brown sugar

# Chocolate and Banana Puddings

**489**

SERVES 4

PREPARATION TIME 40 MINUTES

COOKING TIME 5 MINUTES

### INGREDIENTS

100 ml / 3 ½ fl. oz / ½ cup double (heavy) cream
100 g / 3 ½ oz / ¾ cup milk chocolate, chopped

14 biscuits
1 banana, chopped

- Heat the cream to simmering point then pour it over the chocolate and stir until smooth.
- Put 6 of the biscuits into a food processor and blend to fine crumbs.
- Pour in the chocolate mixture then add the banana and blend again until smooth.
- Divide the mixture between 4 bowls and press 2 biscuits into the top of each one.
- Chill in the fridge for 30 minutes or until firm.

# Coconut Fool

**490**

SERVES 4

PREPARATION TIME 10 MINUTES

COOKING TIME 2 MINUTES

### INGREDIENTS

75 g / 2 ½ oz / ¾ cup desiccated coconut
300 ml / 10 ½ fl. oz / 1 ¼ cups double (heavy) cream

300 g / 10 ½ oz / 1 ¼ cups coconut flavoured yoghurt (yogurt)

- Preheat the grill to its highest setting.
- Spread the coconut out on a baking sheet and toast under the hot grill until golden brown. Leave to cool.
- Whip the cream until thick but not stiff, then fold in the yoghurt and half of the toasted coconut.
- Spoon the cream into 4 fool glasses and sprinkle over the remaining coconut.

**491**

SERVES 4

# Crêpes with Chocolate Drizzle

PREPARATION TIME 10 MINUTES

COOKING TIME 20 MINUTES

## INGREDIENTS

150 g / 5 ½ oz / 1 cup plain (all purpose) flour
1 large egg
325 ml / 11 ½ fl. oz / 1 ⅓ cup whole milk
30 g / 1 oz butter, melted

### FOR THE DRIZZLE
100 ml / 3 ½ fl. oz / ½ cup double (heavy) cream
1 tbsp brandy
100 g / 3 ½ oz / ¾ cup dark chocolate (minimum 60 % cocoa solids), chopped

### FOR THE TOPPINGS
1 orange, zest finely grated
1 tbsp desiccated coconut
1 tbsp crystallised ginger, chopped
1 tbsp chocolate honeycomb, crushed

- To make the chocolate drizzle, heat the cream and brandy to simmering point then pour it over the chocolate and stir to emulsify. Set aside.
- Sieve the flour into a bowl and make a well in the centre. Break in the egg and pour in the milk then use a whisk to incorporate all of the flour from round the outside.
- Melt the butter in a frying pan then whisk it into the batter. Put the buttered frying pan back over a low heat. Add a small ladle of batter and swirl to coat the bottom.
- When it starts to dry and curl up at the edges, turn the pancake over with a spatula and cook the other side until golden brown and cooked through.
- Repeat with the rest of the mixture then roll up the crêpes and arrange them on a serving platter.
- Drizzle over the chocolate sauce and sprinkle with the toppings of your choice.

## Crêpes with White Chocolate Drizzle

**492**

- Replace the dark chocolate with white chocolate and cook the same way.

**493**

SERVES 2

# Sweet French Toast

PREPARATION TIME 5 MINUTES

COOKING TIME 4 MINUTES

## INGREDIENTS

1 orange, zest finely grated
2 large eggs
75 ml / 2 ½ fl. oz / ⅓ cup milk
25 g / 1 oz butter
8 slices baguette
4 tbsp runny honey

- Whisk the orange zest into the eggs with the milk.
- Heat the butter in a large frying pan until sizzling.
- Dip the baguette slices in the egg mixture on both sides until evenly coated then fry them for 2 minutes on each side or until golden brown. Divide the toast between 2 plates.
- Drizzle the toasts with honey and serve immediately.

## Marmalade French Toast

**494**

- Replace the honey with marmalade and heat it in a small pan until runny.

**495**

**SERVES 2**

# Baked Bananas with Rum and Raisins

- Preheat the oven to 180⁰C (160⁰C fan) / 355F / gas 4.
- Arrange the bananas in a small baking dish.
- Scrape the seeds out of the vanilla pod into a small bowl and mix with the honey and rum.
- Spoon over the bananas and scatter over the raisins and sultanas, along with the vanilla pod.
- Bake in the oven for 10 minutes or until the bananas are soft and the liquid has thickened.

PREPARATION TIME 5 MINUTES

COOKING TIME 10 MINUTES

### INGREDIENTS

2 bananas, halved lengthways
1 vanilla pod, halved lengthways
2 tbsp runny honey
2 tbsp dark rum
3 tbsp raisins and sultanas

### Baked Bananas with Chocolate

 **496**

- Omit the raisins and sultanas. Break 100 g / 3 ½ oz / ½ cup of milk chocolate into squares and use them to stud the bananas before baking.

**497**

**SERVES 6**

# Baked Spiced Apples

- Preheat the oven to 180⁰C (160⁰C fan) / 355F gas 4.
- Arrange the apples in a baking dish.
- Beat together the butter, sugar and powdered spices and spread it over the apples, then scatter over the whole spices.
- Bake in the oven for 25 minutes or until the apples are soft.

PREPARATION TIME 10 MINUTES

COOKING TIME 25 MINUTES

### INGREDIENTS

6 small eating apples, peeled
2 tbsp butter, softened
2 tbsp brown sugar
½ tsp ground ginger
½ tsp ground cinnamon
1 vanilla pod
1 cinnamon stick
1 orange, zest peeled

### Mincemeat Stuffed Apples

 **498**

- Core the apples and stuff each cavity with a heaped teaspoon of mincemeat.

499

SERVES 6

# Fresh Fruit Sponge Pudding

PREPARATION TIME 10 MINUTES

COOKING TIME 30–35 MINUTES

### INGREDIENTS

110 g / 4 oz / ⅔ cup self-raising flour, sifted
110 g / 4 oz / ½ cup caster (superfine) sugar
110 g / 4 oz / ½ cup butter, softened
2 large eggs
1 tsp vanilla extract
2 plums, cut into eighths
55 g / 2 oz / ⅓ cup raspberries
55 g / 2 oz / ⅓ cup seedless black grapes

- Preheat the oven to 190°C (170°C fan) / 375F / gas 5 and butter a small baking dish.
- Combine the flour, sugar, butter, eggs and vanilla extract in a bowl and whisk together for 2 minutes or until smooth.
- Arrange half of the fruit in the baking dish and spoon in the cake mixture.
- Top with the rest of the fruit then bake for 30–35 minutes.
- Test with a wooden toothpick, if it comes out clean, the cake is done.
- Serve warm with custard or cream.

## Blueberry Sponge Pudding

500

- Replace the fruit with 200 g / 7 oz / 1 ⅓ cups of fresh blueberries and add the grated zest of an orange to the cake batter.

501

SERVES 2

# Coffee Ice Cream Sundae

PREPARATION TIME 10 MINUTES

### INGREDIENTS

150 ml / 5 ½ fl. oz / ⅔ cup double (heavy) cream
2 shots fresh espresso
2 scoops of vanilla ice cream
2 scoops of coffee ice cream
4 chocolated-coated stick biscuits
chocolate sprinkles and cocoa powder to garnish

- Whip the cream until thick then spoon it into a piping bag fitted with a large star nozzle.
- Put an espresso shot in the bottom of 2 glass mugs and top with a scoop of vanilla ice cream.
- Scoop in some coffee ice cream then pipe a swirl of cream on top of each one.
- Garnish the sundaes with 2 chocolate-coated stick biscuits, chocolate sprinkles and a dusting of cocoa powder.

## Tiramisu Sundae

502

- Break 8 sponge fingers into pieces and divide between the mugs before topping with the espresso and a shot of coffee liqueur.

**503**

**SERVES 4**

# Summer Fruit Crumble

- Preheat the oven to 180°C (160°C fan) / 355F / gas 4.
- Mix the fruit with the sugar and tip it into a baking dish.
- Rub the butter into the flour and stir in the ground almonds and brown sugar.
- Take a handful of the topping and squeeze it into a clump, then crumble it over the fruit.
- Repeat with the rest of the crumble mixture then bake for 40 minutes or until the topping is golden brown.

PREPARATION TIME 5 MINUTES

COOKING TIME 40 MINUTES

**INGREDIENTS**

300 g / 10 ½ oz / 2 cups mixed summer fruit
4 tbsp caster (superfine) sugar
75 g / 2 ½ oz / ⅓ cup butter
50 g / 1 ¾ oz / ⅓ cup plain (all purpose) flour
25 g / 1 oz / ¼ cup ground almonds
40 g / 1 ½ oz / ¼ cup light brown sugar

## Summer Fruit Cobbler

**504**

- Add enough milk to the crumble mixture to bring it together into a soft dough. Shape it into small discs and arrange them round the outside of the baking dish before baking.

**505**

**SERVES 6**

# Raspberry and Vanilla Trifle Pots

- Scrape the seeds out of the vanilla pod and put them in a small saucepan with the milk. Bring to a simmer then turn off the heat and leave to infuse for 5 minutes.
- Whisk the egg yolks, sugar and cornflour together then gradually whisk in the milk.
- Scrape the mixture back into the saucepan then cook over a medium heat until the mixture thickens, stirring constantly. Remove from the heat and plunge the base of the pan into cold water.
- Mash a third of the raspberries with a fork then stir in the rest of the whole raspberries.
- Put a spoonful of the raspberry mixture in the bottom of 6 glasses and crumble over half of the cake.
- Top with half the custard, then add half of the remaining raspberries. Top with the rest of the cake, then the rest of the custard and finish each glass with a ring of raspberries.

PREPARATION TIME 20 MINUTES

COOKING TIME 15–20 MINUTES

**INGREDIENTS**

200 g / 7 oz / 1 ¾ cup raspberries
1 small Madeira loaf cake

FOR THE CUSTARD
1 vanilla pod, split lengthways
450 ml / 16 fl. oz / 1 ¾ cup whole milk
4 large egg yolks
75 g / 2 ½ oz / ½ cup caster (superfine) sugar
2 tsp cornflour (cornstarch)

## Strawberry and Vanilla Trifle Pots

**506**

- Replace the raspberries with strawberries.

507

SERVES 8

# Pineapple Tarte Tatin

## Apricot Tarte Tatin

508

• Replace the pineapple with canned apricot halves.

## Mandarin Tarte Tatin

509

• Replace the pineapple with canned mandarin segments.

PREPARATION TIME 10 MINUTES

COOKING TIME 25 MINUTES

### INGREDIENTS

2 tbsp butter, softened and cubed
3 tbsp dark brown sugar
400 g / 14 oz / 2 cups canned pineapple rings, drained
250 g / 9 oz all-butter puff pastry

• Preheat the oven to 220°C (200°C fan) / 430F / gas 7.
• Dot the butter over the base of a large ovenproof frying pan and sprinkle over the sugar.
• Arrange the pineapple rings on top.
• Roll out the pastry on a floured surface and cut out a circle slightly larger than the frying pan.
• Lay the pastry over the pineapple and tuck in the edges, then prick a hole in the centre and transfer the pan to the oven and bake for 25 minutes or until the pastry is golden brown and cooked through.
• Using oven gloves, put a large plate on top of the frying pan and turn them both over in one smooth movement to unmould the tart.

510

SERVES 4

# Summer Fruits with Mint Cream

- Mix the strawberries with the raspberries in a shallow bowl.
- Put the honey, lemon juice and mint in a small saucepan with 2 tablespoons of water and bring to a simmer.
- Pour the marinade over the fruit and leave to macerate for 35 minutes.
- Meanwhile, whip the cream with the icing sugar until thick then spoon it into a piping bag fitted with a large star nozzle.
- Discard the mint sprigs and divide the fruit between 4 sundae glasses.
- Pipe a swirl of cream on top of each one and sprinkle over the chopped mint.

PREPARATION TIME 35 MINUTES

COOKING TIME 5 MINUTES

### INGREDIENTS

200 g / 7 oz / 1 cup strawberries
100 g / 3 ½ oz / ⅔ cup raspberries
2 tbsp runny honey
2 tbsp lemon juice
2 sprigs mint

### FOR THE CREAM
300 ml / 10 ½ fl. oz / 1 ¼ cups double (heavy) cream
2 tbsp icing (confectioners') sugar
1 tbsp mint, finely chopped

### Summer Fruits with Basil and Lime Cream

511

- Replace the mint with fresh basil and replace the lemon juice with lime juice.

512

SERVES 4

# Pineapple and Raspberry Salad

- Put the honey, rum and peppercorns in a small saucepan with 4 tbsp water and infuse over a low heat for 5 minutes.
- Arrange the pineapple in a serving bowl and pour over the mixture, then leave to marinate for 20 minutes.
- Scatter the raspberries over the pineapple and garnish with mint leaves and a dusting of icing sugar.

PREPARATION TIME 25 MINUTES

COOKING TIME 5 MINUTES

### INGREDIENTS

4 tbsp honey
2 tbsp dark rum
½ tsp Szechuan peppercorns
1 pineapple, peeled, cored and cut into chunks
150 g / 5 ½ oz / 1 ¼ cups raspberries
mint leaves and icing (confectioners') sugar to garnish

### Pineapple and Blueberry Salad

513

- Replace the raspberries with blueberries.

**514**

SERVES 8

# Apple and Lemon Tarte Tatin

PREPARATION TIME 10 MINUTES

COOKING TIME 25 MINUTES

### INGREDIENTS

2 tbsp butter, softened and cubed
3 tbsp dark brown sugar
1 lemon, juiced and zest finely grated
4 Bramley apples, peeled and thinly sliced
250 g / 9 oz all-butter puff pastry
whipped cream and finely pared lemon zest to serve

- Preheat the oven to 220⁰C (200⁰C fan) / 430F / gas 7.
- Beat together the butter, sugar and lemon zest and juice then mix in the apple slices.
- Spread the mixture out inside an oven proof frying pan.
- Roll out the pastry on a floured surface and cut out a circle slightly larger than the frying pan.
- Lay the pastry over the apples and tuck in the edges, then prick in several places with a sharp knife and transfer the pan to the oven and bake for 25 minutes or until the pastry is golden brown and cooked through.
- Using oven gloves, put a large plate on top of the frying pan and turn them both over in one smooth movement to unmould the tart.
- Cut into slices and serve with a spoonful of whipped cream and a sprinkling of lemon zest.

### Apple and Lavender Tarte Tatin

 515

- Add ½ tsp of dried lavender flowers to the butter and sugar mixture.

**516**

SERVES 4

# Pink Grapefruit with Mint and Gin

PREPARATION TIME 30 MINUTES

COOKING TIME 4 MINUTES

### INGREDIENTS

3 tbsp runny honey
3 tbsp gin
1 tbsp mint, finely chopped
2 pink grapefruit, cut into segments

- Put the honey, gin and mint in a small saucepan with 3 tbsp water and bring to a simmer.
- Pour the mixture over the grapefruit segments and leave to marinate for 30 minutes.
- Divide the grapefruit between 4 glasses and serve chilled or at room temperature.

### Pink Grapefruit and Gin Sorbet

 517

- Blend the grapefruit and gin syrup in a food processor until smooth, then churn in an ice cream machine for 25 minutes or until firm.

**518**

**SERVES 4**

# Chocolate Risotto

- Heat the milk in a saucepan with 500 ml / 18 fl. oz / 2 cups water.
- Heat the butter in a sauté pan and stir in the rice, cocoa and sugar.
- When the rice is well coated with the butter, add 2 ladles of the hot milk.
- Cook, stirring occasionally, until most of the milk has been absorbed before adding the next 2 ladles.
- Continue in this way for around 15 minutes or until the rice is just tender.
- Stir in the chocolate and crème fraîche, then cover the pan and take off the heat to rest for 4 minutes.
- Stir well then spoon into glass mugs and serve immediately.

PREPARATION TIME 5 MINUTES

COOKING TIME 25 MINUTES

......................................................

### INGREDIENTS

500 ml / 18 fl. oz / 2 cups milk
4 tbsp butter
150 g / 5 ½ oz / ¾ cup risotto rice
3 tbsp unsweetened cocoa powder
4 tbsp caster (superfine) sugar
50 g / 1 ¾ oz / ⅓ cup dark chocolate (minimum 60 % cocoa solids), grated
2 tbsp crème fraîche

## Chocolate and Almond Risotto

 **519**

- Cut 200 g / 7 oz / ½ cup of marzipan into small cubes and stir it into the risotto with the chocolate and crème fraîche.

**520**

**SERVES 4**

# Vanilla Baked Peaches

- Preheat the oven to 180°C (160°C fan) / 355F / gas 4.
- Arrange the peaches, cut side up, in 4 small baking dishes.
- Scrape the seeds out of the vanilla pod and put them in a small saucepan with the honey and orange juice. Bring to a simmer then pour the liquid over the peaches.
- Bake in the oven for 25 minutes or until the peaches are soft.
- Serve garnished with the empty vanilla pod.

PREPARATION TIME 10 MINUTES

COOKING TIME 25–30 MINUTES

......................................................

### INGREDIENTS

6 peaches, halved and stoned
1 vanilla pod, split lengthways
2 tbsp runny honey
1 orange, juiced

## Lavender Baked Peaches

 **521**

- Replace the vanilla pod with 2 sprigs of dried lavender.

# White Chocolate Fondue

PREPARATION TIME 5 MINUTES

COOKING TIME 4 MINUTES

......................................................

### INGREDIENTS

100 g / 3 ½ oz / ⅔ cup white
chocolate
150 ml / 3 ½ fl. oz / ⅔ cup double
(heavy) cream
2 tbsp Cointreau
raspberries and brownie squares
for dipping

- Chop the chocolate and put it in a fondue bowl.
- Bring the cream and Cointreau to simmering point
  then pour it over the chocolate and stir until smooth.
- Serve with the raspberries and brownie squares for
  dipping.

## White Chocolate Espresso Fondue

523

- Replace the Cointreau with coffee liqueur
  and add 2 shots of espresso to the cream.

524
SERVES 6

# Lemon Curd Ice Cream Tart

PREPARATION TIME 50 MINUTES

......................................................

### INGREDIENTS

1 jar lemon curd
1 ready-made pastry case
450 g / 1 lb / 1 ¾ cup lemon curd ice
cream, slightly softened
candied lemon peel, to garnish

- Spoon the lemon curd into the pastry case and level the
  surface.
- Scoop in the ice cream and level the top with a palette
  knife, then transfer the tart to the freezer for 40
  minutes.
- Meanwhile, cut the candied peel into long thin strips,
  then cut half of it across into tiny cubes.
- Take the tart out of the freezer and sprinkle with
  candied peel, then serve immediately.

## Strawberry Ice Cream Tart

525

- Replace the lemon curd with strawberry
  jam (jelly) and substitute strawberry ice
  cream for the lemon curd ice cream.

**526**

SERVES 4

# Mulled Wine Pears

## Mulled Cider Pears

 **527**

- Replace the wine with cider.

## Mulled Port Pears

 **528**

- Replace half of the wine with port.

PREPARATION TIME 5 MINUTES

COOKING TIME 40 MINUTES

### INGREDIENTS

700 ml / 1 pint 4 fl. oz / 3 ½ cups red wine
100 g / 3 ½ oz / ½ cup caster (superfine) sugar
1 orange, juiced
2 cinnamon sticks
4 cloves
a few sprigs thyme, plus extra to garnish
8 small ripe pears, peeled

- Put the wine, sugar, orange juice, spices and thyme in a large saucepan and bring to the boil, stirring to dissolve the sugar.
- Boil for 5 minutes then add the pears and simmer for 30 minutes, or until tender.
- Arrange the pears in a serving dish then strain the sauce through a sieve to remove the spices and pour it over the top.
- Garnish the pears with fresh thyme sprigs and serve hot or cold.

**SERVES 4**

# Crêpes Suzette

PREPARATION TIME 10 MINUTES

COOKING TIME 30 MINUTES

## INGREDIENTS

150 g / 5 ½ oz / 1 cup plain (all purpose) flour
1 large egg
325 ml / 11 ½ fl. oz / 1 ¼ cups whole milk
30 g / 1 oz butter, melted
2 oranges, juiced and zest finely pared
1 lemon, juiced
4 tbsp caster (superfine) sugar
2 tbsp Cointreau

- Sieve the flour into a bowl and make a well in the centre. Break in the egg and pour in the milk then use a whisk to incorporate all of the flour from round the outside.
- Melt the butter in a frying pan then whisk it into the batter. Put the buttered frying pan back over a low heat. Add a small ladle of batter and swirl to coat the bottom.
- When it starts to dry and curl up at the edges, turn the pancake over with a spatula and cook the other side until golden brown and cooked through.
- Repeat with the rest of the mixture then fold the crêpes into quarters. Put the rest of the ingredients in the pan and heat until bubbling, stirring to dissolve the sugar.
- Arrange the folded pancakes in the pan and cook for 30 seconds, then turn them over and cook for another 30 seconds so that they soak up some of the sauce.
- Transfer the crêpes to warm plates and spoon over any leftover sauce.

## Lemon Crêpes

 530

- Replace the oranges with lemons and the Cointreau with Limoncello.

531

**MAKES 6**

# Muesli Biscuits

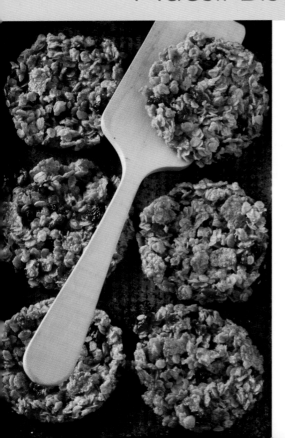

PREPARATION TIME 10 MINUTES

COOKING TIME 20–25 MINUTES

## INGREDIENTS

100 g / 3 ½ oz / ¼ cup butter
100 g / 3 ½ oz / ½ cup light brown sugar
300 g / 10 ½ oz / 2 ½ cups fruit and nut muesli

- Preheat the oven to 170°C (150°C fan) / 340F / gas 3
- Put the butter and sugar in a small saucepan and heat together until melted, stirring to dissolve the sugar. Stir in the muesli.
- When the mixture is cool enough to handle, press it into 6 patties with your hands and space them out on a baking tray.
- Bake for 20–25 minutes or until the biscuits are firm and lightly golden on top.

## Oat and Marzipan Biscuits

 532

- Replace the muesli with porridge oats and add 100 g / 3 ½ oz / ½ cup of marzipan in small cubes.

533

SERVES 4

# Apple and Cinnamon Bread Pudding

- Preheat the oven to 180°C (160°C fan) / 355F / gas 4.
- Spread the bread with butter and cut it into triangles.
- Mix the Demerara sugar with the cinnamon then stir in the apple and Calvados.
- Spread the apple mixture over the bread triangles then arrange them in a baking dish.
- Whisk the milk, cream, eggs and caster sugar together and pour it over the top, then press down on the bread to help it soak up the liquid.
- Bake for 35–40 minutes or until the top is golden brown.

PREPARATION TIME 15 MINUTES

COOKING TIME 35–40 MINUTES

**INGREDIENTS**

1 loaf white bread, sliced and crusts removed
3 tbsp butter, softened
2 tbsp Demerara sugar
1 tsp ground cinnamon
1 Bramley apple, grated
1 tbsp Calvados
250 ml / 9 fl. oz / 1 cup whole milk
200 ml / 7 oz / ¾ cup double (heavy) cream
4 large egg yolks
75 g / 2 ½ oz / ⅓ cup caster (superfine) sugar

## Apple and Almond Pudding

 534

- Replace the Calvados with Amaretto and sprinkle the pudding with 50 g / 2 oz / ⅓ cup of flaked (slivered) almonds before baking.

535

SERVES 2

# Caramelised Spiced Mangoes

- Preheat the oven to 180°C (160°C fan) / 355F / gas 4.
- Arrange the mango wedges in a small baking dish.
- Mix the honey with the rum, melted butter and star anise and pour it over the top.
- Bake in the oven for 15 minutes or until the mango is soft and starting to caramelise at the edges.

PREPARATION TIME 5 MINUTES

COOKING TIME 15 MINUTES

**INGREDIENTS**

2 mangoes, peeled, stoned and cut into wedges
3 tbsp runny honey
2 tbsp dark rum
1 tbsp butter, melted
2 star anise

## Spiced Mango Sorbet

 536

- Spoon the finished mangoes into a food processor and blend until smooth then churn in an ice cream machine for 25 minutes or until firm.

**537**

**SERVES 6-8**

# Watermelon Salad

## Tropical Fruits with Chilli Salt

**538**

- Put ½ tsp of chilli (chili) flakes and 2 tsp sea salt crystals in a pestle and mortar and crush to a powder. Serve with the fruit for dipping.

## Watermelon Sorbet Bowl

**539**

- Use the hollowed out watermelon as a bowl for serving scoops of tropical fruit sorbet.

**PREPARATION TIME 25 MINUTES**

### INGREDIENTS

½ seedless watermelon
2 tbsp caster (superfine) sugar
2 limes, juiced
2 peaches, cubed
2 apples, cubed
2 pears, cubed
lemon verbena leaves to serve

- Scoop the centre out of the watermelon and cut the flesh into cubes.
- Combine the sugar and lime juice in a small bowl and stir to dissolve.
- Mix the watermelon cubes with the rest of the fruit then toss with the lime juice and pack back into the watermelon shell.
- Garnish with lemon verbena and serve with wooden skewers to eat the fruit with.

**540**

SERVES 4

# Espresso Risotto

- Heat the milk in a saucepan with 500 ml / 18 fl. oz / 2 cups water and the vanilla extract.
- Heat the butter in a sauté pan and stir in the sugar and rice.
- When the rice is well coated with the butter, add 2 ladles of the hot milk.
- Cook, stirring occasionally, until most of the milk has been absorbed before adding the next 2 ladles.
- Continue in this way for around 15 minutes or until the rice is just tender.
- Stir in the crème fraîche, then cover the pan and take off the heat to rest for 4 minutes.
- Spoon into 4 glasses and pour an espresso shot over each one. Serve immediately.

**PREPARATION TIME 5 MINUTES**

**COOKING TIME 25 MINUTES**

**INGREDIENTS**

500 ml / 18 fl. oz / 2 cups milk
1 tsp vanilla extract
4 tbsp butter
50 g / 1 ¾ oz / ¼ cup caster (superfine) sugar
150 g / 5 ½ oz / ¾ cup risotto rice
2 tbsp crème fraîche
4 shots espresso

### Chocolate and Espresso Risotto

**541**

- Add 1 tbsp of cocoa powder to the rice and stir in 75 g / 3 oz / ¾ cup of grated chocolate with the crème fraîche at the end.

**542**

SERVES 4

# Chocolate and Almond Sponge Pudding

- Preheat the oven to 190°C (170°C fan) / 375F / gas 5 and butter a small baking dish.
- Combine the flour, cocoa, sugar, butter, eggs and almond extract in a bowl and whisk together for 2 minutes or until smooth.
- Spoon it into the baking dish and sprinkle with flaked almonds then bake for 30–35 minutes.
- Test with a wooden toothpick, if it comes out clean, the cake is done.
- Serve warm with custard or cream.

**PREPARATION TIME 10 MINUTES**

**COOKING TIME 30–35 MINUTES**

**INGREDIENTS**

110 g / 4 oz / ⅔ cup self-raising flour, sifted
3 tbsp unsweetened cocoa powder
110 g / 4 oz / ½ cup caster (superfine) sugar
110 g / 4 oz / ½ cup butter, softened
2 large eggs
1 tsp almond extract
2 tbsp flaked (slivered) almonds

### Chocolate and Orange Sponge Pudding

**543**

- Omit the almonds and almond extract and replace with the grated zest of an orange and 1 tbsp Cointreau.

# Summer Fruit Cheesecake Pots

PREPARATION TIME 40 MINUTES

COOKING TIME 5 MINUTES

### INGREDIENTS

200 g / 7 oz / ¾ cup cream cheese
200 g / 7 oz / 1 cup condensed milk
2 lemons, juiced
200 g / 7 oz / 1 cup mixed summer
berries
redcurrant sprigs to serve

### FOR THE CHOCOLATE SAUCE

100 ml / 3 ½ fl. oz / ½ cup double
(heavy) cream
1 tbsp brandy
75 g / 2 ½ oz / ¾ cup dark chocolate
(minimum 60 % cocoa solids),
chopped

- Beat the cream cheese with an electric whisk until smooth then whisk in the condensed milk.
- Whisk in the lemon juice until the mixture starts to thicken, then fold in the berries and spoon into 4 glasses.
- Leave to chill in the fridge for 30 minutes to firm up.
- Meanwhile, make the chocolate sauce.
- Heat the cream and brandy to simmering point then pour it over the chocolate and stir to emulsify.
- When the pots have set, drizzle over some of the sauce and serve immediately, topped with redcurrant sprigs.

# Chocolate Ice Cream Biscuits

PREPARATION TIME 30 MINUTES

COOKING TIME 4 MINUTES

### INGREDIENTS

200 g / 7 oz / 2 cups dark chocolate
(minimum 60 % cocoa solids),
chopped
6 ginger nut biscuits
6 scoops vanilla ice cream

- Line a small baking tray with a non-stick making mat.
- Melt the chocolate in a microwave or bain marie.
- Dip the biscuits in the chocolate and space them out, chocolate side down, on the baking tray.
- Freeze for 5 minutes to set the chocolate.
- Take the tray out of the freezer and add a big scoop of ice cream to the top of each biscuit.
- Spoon over the slightly cooled chocolate to cover the ice cream completely, then put the tray back in the freezer for 15 minutes.

**546**

**SERVES 6**

# Chocolate and Raspberry Parfaits

- Line 6 mini pudding basins with cling film.
- Mix the softened ice cream with the raspberries and pistachio nuts and pack the mixture into the pudding basins.
- Freeze the parfaits for 30 minutes or until firm.
- Turn the parfaits out onto serving plates and peel off the clingfilm then garnish with extra raspberries and pistachios.

**PREPARATION TIME 45 MINUTES**

.........................................................

### INGREDIENTS

450 g / 1 lb / 1 ¾ cup chocolate ice cream, softened slightly
100 g / 3 ½ oz / ¾ cup raspberries
50 g / 2 ½ oz / ½ cup pistachio nuts, chopped

# Mini Pavlovas with Fruit Coulis

**547**

**SERVES 4**

**PREPARATION TIME 35 MINUTES**

**COOKING TIME 5 MINUTES**

.........................................................

### INGREDIENTS

250 g / 10 ½ oz / 1 ¼ cups mixed summer berries
2 tbsp caster (superfine) sugar
1 tbsp kirsch

250 ml / 9 fl. oz / 1 cup double (heavy) cream
4 meringue nests
mint leaves to garnish

- Reserve some of the berries for a garnish and put the rest in a saucepan with the sugar and kirsch.
- Cook over a low heat for 5 minutes or until the berries start to burst.
- Pour the mixture into a liquidiser and blend to a smooth sauce then chill in the fridge for 25 minutes.
- Whisk the cream until softly whipped and spoon it onto the meringue nests.
- Arrange the mini pavlovas on a serving plate and drizzle the coulis over and around.
- Scatter over the berries and garnish with mint leaves.

# Blueberry Yoghurt Pots

**548**

**SERVES 4**

**PREPARATION TIME 5 MINUTES**

.........................................................

### INGREDIENTS

400 g / 14 oz / 1 ⅔ cups blueberry yoghurt
100 g / 3 ½ oz / 1 cup granola
4 tbsp condensed milk
50 g / 1 ¾ oz / ⅓ cup blueberries

- Divide half the yoghurt between 4 glasses and top with the granola.
- Top with the rest of the yoghurt, then add a tablespoon of condensed milk to each one and sprinkle over the blueberries.

## 549
### SERVES 4

# Passion Fruit and Lemon Cheesecake Pots

PREPARATION TIME 40 MINUTES

### INGREDIENTS

200 g / 7 oz / ¾ cup cream cheese
200 g / 7 oz / 1 cup condensed milk
2 lemons, juiced
1 tbsp poppy seeds
4 passion fruit, halved

- Beat the cream cheese with an electric whisk until smooth then whisk in the condensed milk.
- Whisk in the lemon juice and poppy seeds until the mixture starts to thicken, then spoon into 4 glasses.
- Leave to chill in the fridge for 30 minutes to firm up.
- When the pots have set, spoon over the passion fruit pulp and seeds and serve.

### Kiwi Cheesecake Pots
- Replace the passion fruit with 3 finely chopped kiwi fruits.

550

## 551
### SERVES 4

# Peach Crumble

PREPARATION TIME 5 MINUTES

COOKING TIME 40 MINUTES

### INGREDIENTS

3 peaches, peeled, stoned and cubed
75 g / 2 ½ oz / ⅓ cup butter
50 g / 1 ¾ oz / ⅓ cup plain (all purpose) flour
25 g / 1 oz / ¼ cup ground almonds
40 g / 1 ½ oz / ¼ cup light brown sugar

- Preheat the oven to 180°C (160°C fan) / 355F / gas 4.
- Arrange the cubed peaches in a baking dish.
- Rub the butter into the flour and stir in the ground almonds and brown sugar.
- Take a handful of the topping and squeeze it into a clump, then crumble it over the fruit.
- Repeat with the rest of the crumble mixture then bake for 40 minutes or until the topping is golden brown.

### Mango Crumble
- Replace the peaches with 3 peeled, stoned mangoes, cut into cubes.

552

### 553
**SERVES 4**

# Stewed Mirabelles

- Put the wine, sugar, lemon and spices in a saucepan and add 200 ml / 7 fl. oz / ¾ cup water.
- Bring to the boil, stirring to dissolve the sugar then stir in the mirabelles.
- Simmer gently for 15 minutes or until they are soft.
- Serve warm or chilled.

**PREPARATION TIME 5 MINUTES**

**COOKING TIME 20 MINUTES**

### INGREDIENTS

200 ml / 7 fl. oz / ¾ cup white wine
75 g / 2 ½ oz / ⅓ cup caster (superfine) sugar
1 lemon, zest finely pared
1 vanilla pod, slit lengthways
1 cinnamon stick
450 g / 1 lb / 2 ⅔ cup mirabelles

### Stewed Cherries

 554

- Replace the mirabelles with cherries and use orange zest instead of lemon zest.

### 555
**SERVES 4**

# Nectarine and Apricot Crumble

- Preheat the oven to 180°C (160°C fan) / 355F / gas 4.
- Arrange the nectarines and dried apricots in a baking dish.
- Rub the butter into the flour and stir in the ground almonds and brown sugar.
- Take a handful of the topping and squeeze it into a clump, then crumble it over the fruit.
- Repeat with the rest of the crumble mixture then bake for 40 minutes or until the topping is golden brown.

**PREPARATION TIME 5 MINUTES**

**COOKING TIME 40 MINUTES**

### INGREDIENTS

3 nectarines, peeled, stoned and cubed
50 g / 1 ¾ oz / ¼ cup dried apricots, chopped
75 g / 2 ½ oz / ⅓ cup butter
50 g / 1 ¾ oz / ⅓ cup plain (all purpose) flour
25 g / 1 oz / ¼ cup ground almonds
40 g / 1 ½ oz / ¼ cup light brown sugar

### Double Apricot Crumble

 556

- Replace the nectarines with fresh apricots.

### 557
**SERVES 6**

# Chocolate Samosas with Pineapple

PREPARATION TIME 25 MINUTES

COOKING TIME 12–15 MINUTES

........................................................

### INGREDIENTS

225 g / 8 oz filo pastry
100 g / 3 ½ oz / ½ cup butter, melted
200 g / 7 oz / 2 cups dark chocolate (minimum 60 % cocoa solids), finely chopped
1 pineapple, peeled and thinly sliced

- Preheat the oven to 180°C (160°C fan) / 355F / gas 4 and grease a large baking tray.
- Cut the pile of filo sheets in half then take one halved sheet and brush it with melted butter.
- Arrange a tablespoon of chopped chocolate at one end and fold the corner over, then triangle-fold it up.
- Transfer the samosa to the baking tray and repeat with the rest of the filo and chocolate, then brush with any leftover butter.
- Arrange the pineapple slices alongside the samosas and roast for 12–15 minutes or until the pastry is crisp and the pineapple is caramelised at the edges.
- Serve warm.

### Chocolate Orange Samosas
 558

- Add the grated zest of an orange to the chopped chocolate and add 1 tbsp of Cointreau to the melted butter.

### 559
**SERVES 6**

# Fig and Raspberry Compote

PREPARATION TIME 10 MINUTES

COOKING TIME 8 MINUTES

........................................................

### INGREDIENTS

250 g / 5 oz / 2 cups raspberries
4 figs, quartered
1 orange, juiced and zest finely grated
2 tbsp light brown sugar
200 ml / 7 fl. oz / ¾ cup double (heavy) cream
2 tbsp icing (confectioners') sugar
1 tsp vanilla extract

- Preheat the oven to 200°C (180°C fan) / 390F / gas 6.
- Put the fruit in a saucepan with the orange juice and zest and brown sugar.
- Cover with a lid and cook over a medium heat for 8 minutes, stirring occasionally, then spoon the compote into 6 bowls or glasses.
- Whip the cream with the icing sugar and vanilla extract until thick then spoon on top of the compotes.

### Fig and Rhubarb Compote
 560

- Replace the raspberries with 3 chopped rhubarb stems.

**561**

SERVES 4

# Natural Yoghurt with Summer Fruit Coulis

## Natural Yoghurt with Lemon Sauce

**562**

- Make a simple sauce by mixing 2 tbsp of limoncello with 4 tbsp of lemon curd. Drizzle over the yoghurts and garnish with fresh raspberries.

## Fromage Frais with Summer Fruit Coulis

**563**

- Replace the yoghurt with unsweetened fromage frais and add the grated zest of an orange to the fruits before cooking.

PREPARATION TIME 30 MINUTES

COOKING TIME 5 MINUTES

### INGREDIENTS

250 g / 10 ½ oz / 2 ¼ cups mixed summer berries
2 tbsp caster (superfine) sugar
1 tbsp kirsch
4 pots set natural yoghurt
2 tbsp pistachio nuts, chopped

- Reserve some of the berries for a garnish and put the rest in a saucepan with the sugar and kirsch.
- Cook over a low heat for 5 minutes or until the berries start to burst.
- Pour the mixture into a liquidiser and blend to a smooth sauce then chill in the fridge for 25 minutes.
- Remove the lids from the yoghurt pots and turn them out onto 4 plates.
- Spoon over the cooled coulis and garnish with the rest of the berries and a sprinkling of pistachio nuts.

564

MAKES 4

# Banana and Sultana Bread Puddings

## Apricot Bread Puddings

 565

- Replace the sultanas with chopped dried apricot and substitute the bananas with halved fresh apricots.

## Banana and Rum Puddings

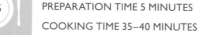 566

- Omit the sultanas and stir 3 tbsp of dark rum into the cream mixture.

PREPARATION TIME 5 MINUTES

COOKING TIME 35–40 MINUTES

### INGREDIENTS

250 ml / 9 fl. oz / 1 cup whole milk
200 ml / 7 fl. oz / ¾ cup double (heavy) cream
4 large egg yolks
75 g / 2 ½ oz / ⅓ cup caster (superfine) sugar
1 loaf white bread, cubed
4 tbsp sultanas
1 tsp mixed spice
2 bananas, quartered
4 tbsp runny honey

- Preheat the oven to 180°C (160°C fan) / 355F / gas 4.
- Whisk the milk, cream, eggs and caster sugar together then stir in the bread, sultanas and spice.
- Divide the mixture between 4 small buttered baking dishes and press 2 pieces of banana into the top of each.
- Bake for 35–40 minutes or until the tops are golden brown, then drizzle over the honey.

**SERVES 4**

# Quick Chocolate Mousse

- Heat the cream to simmering point then pour it over the chocolate and stir until smooth.
- Leave to cool for 10 minutes.
- Whip the egg whites until stiff then whisk in the sugar.
- Stir a big spoonful of the egg white into the cooled chocolate mixture then fold in the rest with a big metal spoon, keeping as many of the air bubbles intact as possible.
- Spoon the mousse into 4 glasses and chill for 20 minutes.
- Decorate with chocolate sugar balls before serving.

PREPARATION TIME 40 MINUTES

COOKING TIME 5 MINUTES

### INGREDIENTS

200 g / 7 fl. oz / ¾ cup double (heavy) cream
200 g / 7 oz / 2 cups milk chocolate, chopped
2 egg whites
4 tbsp caster (superfine) sugar
chocolate sugar balls, to decorate

### Quick White Chocolate Mousse

- Replace the milk chocolate with white chocolate and add the finely grated zest of half an orange.

**SERVES 6**

# Warm Yoghurt Cake with Blueberry Jam

- Preheat the oven to 190°C (170°C fan) / 375F / gas 5 and butter a small baking dish.
- Combine the flour, sugar, yoghurt, eggs and vanilla extract in a bowl and whisk together for 2 minutes or until smooth.
- Spoon the mixture into the baking dish then bake for 30–35 minutes.
- Test with a wooden toothpick, if it comes out clean, the cake is done.
- Towards the end of the cooking time, heat the blueberry jam in a small saucepan with 2 tbsp water until runny.
- Cut the cake into wedges and serve drizzled with the warm jam.

PREPARATION TIME 10 MINUTES

COOKING TIME 30–35 MINUTES

### INGREDIENTS

110 g / 4 oz / ⅔ cup self-raising flour, sifted
110 g / 4 oz / ½ cup caster (superfine) sugar
110 g / 4 oz / ½ cup Greek yoghurt
2 large eggs
1 tsp vanilla extract
1 jar blueberry jam (jelly)

### Warm Citrus Yoghurt Cake

- Add the grated zest of a lemon, a lime and an orange to the cake mixture. Heat 3 tbsp each of lemon curd and marmalade together until runny and drizzle over the cake to serve.

**571**

SERVES 2

# Baked Spiced Bananas

PREPARATION TIME 5 MINUTES

COOKING TIME 15 MINUTES

**INGREDIENTS**

3 bananas, peeled
150 ml / 5 ½ fl. oz / ⅔ cup coconut milk
½ tsp ground cinnamon
½ tsp ground ginger
2 tbsp muscovado sugar
2 tbsp flaked (slivered) almonds

- Preheat the oven to 180°C (160°C fan) / 355F / gas 4.
- Arrange the bananas in a small baking dish and pour over the coconut milk.
- Mix the spices with the brown sugar and sprinkle over the top then scatter over the flaked almonds.
- Bake in the oven for 15 minutes or until the bananas are soft and the liquid has thickened.

### Baked Spiced Mango

**572**

- Replace the bananas with very ripe mango halves that have been peeled and stoned.

**573**

SERVES 4

# Summer Fruit Crêpes

PREPARATION TIME 10 MINUTES

COOKING TIME 20 MINUTES

**INGREDIENTS**

150 g / 5 ½ oz / 1 cup plain (all purpose) flour
1 large egg
325 ml / 11 ½ fl. oz / 1 ½ cups whole milk
30 g / 1 oz butter, melted

FOR THE FILLING

3 tbsp redcurrant jelly
200 g / 7 oz / 1 cup mixed summer berries

- To make the filling, melt the redcurrant jelly in a small saucepan and stir in the fruit. Leave to macerate.
- Sieve the flour into a bowl and make a well in the centre. Break in the egg and pour in the milk then use a whisk to gradually incorporate all of the flour from round the outside.
- Melt the butter in a small frying pan then whisk it into the batter.
- Put the buttered frying pan back over a low heat. Add a small ladle of batter and swirl the pan to coat the bottom.
- When it starts to dry and curl up at the edges, turn the pancake over with a spatula and cook the other side until golden brown and cooked through.
- Repeat with the rest of the mixture then serve each crepe rolled up with a big spoonful of summer fruits inside.

### Winter Fruit Crêpes

**574**

- Use a mixture of dried figs, dried pears and prunes and leave them to macerate in 300 ml / ½ pt / 1 ¼ cups of hot earl grey tea for 30 minutes.

# Index

# Index

# Index